Mastering Flutter and Dart: Elegant Code for Cross-Platform Success

Kameron Hussain and Frahaan Hussain

Published by Sonar Publishing, 2024.

While every precaution has been taken in the preparation of this book, the publisher assumes no responsibility for errors or omissions, or for damages resulting from the use of the information contained herein.

MASTERING FLUTTER AND DART: ELEGANT CODE FOR CROSS-PLATFORM SUCCESS

First edition. March 13, 2024.

ISBN: 979-8224154104

Written by Kameron Hussain and Frahaan Hussain.

Table of Contents

Section 19.4: Emerging Trends in Cross-Platform Development

1. Convergence of Mobile and Desktop

2. Progressive Web Apps (PWAs)

3. Augmented Reality (AR) and Virtual Reality (VR)

4. Internet of Things (IoT)

5. Focus on Performance and Optimization

6. Collaboration and Open Source

7. App Distribution and Monetization

8. Ethical and Sustainable Development

Section 19.5: Preparing for Future Changes in Technology

1. Continuous Learning and Skill Development

2. Embrace New Technologies

3. Community Engagement

4. Experimentation and Prototyping

5. Future-Proofing Code

6. Security and Privacy Awareness

7. Ethical Considerations

8. Environmental Sustainability

9. Adaptability and Resilience

2. Create the Project Structure

3. Implement Navigation

4. Build the User Interface

5. Implement Core Features

6. Integrate Backend Services

7. Manage State Effectively

8. Testing and Debugging

9. Iterate and Refine

10. Performance Optimization

11. Localization and Accessibility

12. Security and Privacy

13. Documentation

14. Version Control and Collaboration

15. Monitor and Track Errors

16. Prepare for Testing and Deployment

17. Finalize MVP and Prepare for Launch

Section 20.3: Integrating Advanced Features

1. Push Notifications

2. In-App Purchases

3. Augmented Reality (AR)

4. Machine Learning

5. Biometric Authentication

6. Augmented Reality (AR)

7. Machine Learning

8. Biometric Authentication

9. Augmented Reality (AR)

10. Machine Learning

11. Biometric Authentication

12. Augmented Reality (AR)

13. Machine Learning

14. Biometric Authentication

15. Augmented Reality (AR)

16. Machine Learning

17. Biometric Authentication

18. Augmented Reality (AR)

Section 20.4: Testing and Refining Your App

1. Unit Testing

2. Widget Testing

3. Integration Testing

4. User Acceptance Testing (UAT)

5. Performance Testing

6. Usability Testing

7. Accessibility Testing

8. Beta Testing

9. Continuous Refinement

10. Documentation and User Support

Section 20.5: Launching and Marketing Your App

1. App Store Submission

2. App Store Optimization (ASO)

3. Social Media Presence

4. App Website and Landing Page

5. Email Marketing

6. Influencer Collaborations

7. App Launch Event

8. User Feedback and Iteration

9. Analytics and Metrics

10. Continuous Marketing Efforts

Chapter 1: Introduction to Flutter and Dart

1.1. The Evolution of Mobile Development: From Native to Cross-Platform

Mobile app development has witnessed a significant transformation over the years. Initially, developers primarily focused on native app development, which involved creating separate codebases for each platform, such as iOS and Android. While this approach allowed for fine-grained control and performance optimization, it was time-consuming and required expertise in multiple programming languages.

With the rise of cross-platform development frameworks, such as Flutter, the landscape has evolved. Cross-platform development aims to streamline the app development process by enabling developers to write code once and run it on multiple platforms. This approach has become increasingly popular due to its efficiency and reduced development overhead.

One of the key factors contributing to the adoption of cross-platform frameworks like Flutter is the demand for faster development cycles. Businesses and developers alike are looking for ways to expedite app development without compromising on quality. Cross-platform solutions address this need by providing a unified codebase that can be deployed across various platforms.

Flutter, introduced by Google, is at the forefront of this cross-platform revolution. It leverages the Dart programming language to build high-quality, natively compiled applications for mobile, web, and desktop from a single codebase. This approach allows developers to reach a broader audience while maintaining a consistent user experience.

The Advantages of Cross-Platform Development

Cross-platform development offers several advantages, which have contributed to its widespread adoption:

1. **Cost-Effective**: Developing a single codebase for multiple platforms reduces development costs and resources compared to maintaining separate codebases.
2. **Time Efficiency**: Cross-platform frameworks like Flutter enable faster development, as developers write code once and deploy it across platforms, reducing development time.
3. **Code Reusability**: Reusing code components across platforms enhances productivity and consistency.
4. **Uniform User Experience**: Users on different platforms receive a consistent user interface and experience, improving user satisfaction.
5. **Easier Maintenance**: Maintaining a single codebase simplifies updates, bug fixes, and feature enhancements.
6. **Wider Reach**: Apps can target both iOS and Android users without the need for separate development efforts.
7. **Community and Support**: Frameworks like Flutter benefit from active communities and extensive libraries, easing the development process.

The Emergence of Flutter

Flutter has gained popularity in the development community due to its unique features and capabilities. It offers a wide range of widgets and tools for building modern, visually appealing user interfaces. Additionally, Flutter provides hot reload functionality, allowing developers to see changes in real-time as they code, greatly accelerating the development process.

Dart, the language behind Flutter, plays a crucial role in its success. It is a versatile, object-oriented language that compiles to native code for high-performance execution. Dart's simplicity and ease of learning make it accessible to both experienced and novice developers.

In the sections that follow, we will delve deeper into Flutter and Dart, exploring their core concepts and how they work together to create cross-platform applications. We will also discuss setting up your development environment to get started with Flutter development. Let's embark on this journey to master Flutter and Dart for modern app development.

1.2. An Overview of Flutter: Revolutionizing UI Development

Flutter, developed by Google, is a powerful open-source UI software development toolkit that is revolutionizing the way we build user interfaces for mobile, web, and desktop applications. It offers a rich set of pre-designed widgets and tools to create stunning and performant applications. In this section, we'll take an in-depth look at what makes Flutter a game-changer in the world of UI development.

A Single Codebase for Multiple Platforms

One of Flutter's standout features is the ability to write a single codebase that can be used to build apps for various platforms, including iOS, Android, web, and desktop. This cross-platform nature significantly reduces development time and effort, as developers no longer need to maintain separate codebases for each platform. The concept of "write once, run anywhere" is at the core of Flutter's philosophy.

```
void main() {
runApp(MyApp());
}
```

The code snippet above is a simple example of a Flutter application's entry point. With minimal platform-specific code, you can create a Flutter app that runs seamlessly on multiple platforms.

Fast Development with Hot Reload

Flutter introduces a feature called "hot reload" that greatly accelerates the development process. Hot reload allows developers to make changes to the code and see the results in real-time, without having to restart the entire application. This feature is invaluable for iterating on the user interface, experimenting with layouts, and fixing bugs on the fly.

```
// Change the text and see it immediately on the screen
Text('Hello, Flutter!');
```

By simply modifying the code and saving the changes, you can witness the updates instantaneously on the emulator or device, enhancing productivity and reducing development cycles.

A Rich Set of Widgets

Flutter offers a comprehensive collection of widgets, ranging from basic building blocks like text and buttons to complex widgets for animations, scrolling, and navigation. Widgets in Flutter are not just for creating user interfaces; they are also for laying out and structuring the application's entire visual hierarchy.

```
class MyWidget extends StatelessWidget {

@override

Widget build(BuildContext context) {

return Scaffold(

appBar: AppBar(

title: Text('Flutter Example'),

),

body: Center(

child: Text('Hello, Flutter!'),

),

);

}

}
```

In this example, the Scaffold, AppBar, and Text widgets are used to create a simple application with a title bar and a centered text element. Flutter's widget-based approach allows for flexible and reusable UI components.

Pixel-Perfect Customization

Flutter empowers developers to achieve pixel-perfect designs and customizations. With its expressive and flexible layout system, you have fine-grained control over every aspect of your app's appearance. Whether you want to create a unique visual style or faithfully replicate a design from a mockup, Flutter provides the tools to achieve your goals.

```
Container(
width: 100,
height: 100,
color: Colors.blue,
child: Center(
child: Text(
'Custom Widget',
style: TextStyle(
color: Colors.white,
fontSize: 16,
),
),
),
)
```

In this code snippet, a custom Container widget is created with specific dimensions, background color, and text style. This level of control enables designers and developers to collaborate closely and bring their creative visions to life.

High Performance and Native-Like Experience

Flutter is designed for high performance, with its applications compiled to native ARM code. This compilation process ensures that Flutter apps deliver near-native performance, resulting in smooth animations and fast response times. Users often can't distinguish between Flutter apps and those built using native development kits.

Flutter's rendering engine, Skia, provides excellent support for 2D graphics and offers a consistent look and feel across platforms. It even adapts to platform-specific design guidelines, making it possible to create apps that feel native on each platform.

Community and Ecosystem

Flutter has a thriving and passionate community of developers, designers, and enthusiasts. This community actively contributes to the ecosystem by creating plugins, packages, and libraries that extend Flutter's capabilities. This extensive library of packages simplifies the integration of various features, such as handling payments, accessing device sensors, or connecting to backend services.

In summary, Flutter has transformed UI development by offering a powerful toolkit that enables developers to create stunning, high-performance applications with a single codebase. Its features, including cross-platform compatibility, hot reload, extensive widget library, customization options, and a vibrant community, make it an ideal choice for modern app development. Whether you're a seasoned developer or new to app development, Flutter provides an exciting platform to bring your ideas to life.

1.3. Dart: The Engine Behind Flutter

Dart is the programming language that powers Flutter and serves as the engine behind this versatile UI toolkit. In this section, we'll explore the key features and concepts of Dart, gaining a fundamental understanding of the language that enables Flutter to deliver high-performance, cross-platform applications.

A Brief Introduction to Dart

Dart is a modern, object-oriented, class-based language developed by Google. It was created with the goal of providing a more productive and scalable alternative for web and app development. Dart was designed to be easy to learn, while also offering powerful features for developers to build efficient and maintainable code.

Dart's Syntax and Structure

Dart's syntax and structure are relatively straightforward, making it accessible to both beginners and experienced developers. Here's a brief overview of some essential aspects of Dart's syntax:

```
// Dart code example

void main() {

var greeting = 'Hello, Dart!';

print(greeting);

}

class Person {

String name;

int age;
```

```
Person(this.name, this.age);

void sayHello() {

print('Hello, my name is $name, and I am $age years old.');

}

}
```

In this example, we define a simple Dart program. We declare a main function as the entry point, create a Person class with constructor and method definitions, and utilize Dart's string interpolation with the $ symbol.

Strongly Typed Language

Dart is a statically and strongly typed language. This means that variable types are determined at compile time and cannot be changed once defined. Dart's type system helps catch errors early in the development process and provides better code documentation.

```
String name = 'Alice';

int age = 30;
```

In this code, we explicitly specify the types of the name and age variables as String and int, respectively. Dart enforces type compatibility and will produce a compile-time error if you attempt to assign a value of the wrong type to a variable.

Object-Oriented Programming

Dart follows object-oriented programming (OOP) principles, making it suitable for building complex software systems. Classes, objects, inheritance, and encapsulation are integral parts of Dart's

OOP model. Here's a simplified example of defining a class and creating an object:

```
class Animal {

String name;

Animal(this.name);

void speak() {

print('$name speaks.');

}

}

void main() {

var dog = Animal('Dog');

dog.speak(); // Output: Dog speaks.

}
```

In this code, we create an Animal class, instantiate an Animal object named dog, and invoke its speak method.

Asynchronous Programming with Futures and Streams

Dart excels in handling asynchronous operations. It provides the Future and Stream classes, which simplify asynchronous programming. Futures represent values or errors that might be available in the future, while Streams represent a sequence of asynchronous events.

```
Future<void> fetchData() async {
```

```
// Simulate fetching data with a delay

await Future.delayed(Duration(seconds: 2));

print('Data fetched successfully.');

}

void main() {

fetchData().then((_) {

print('Operation completed.');

});

}
```

In this example, the fetchData function simulates fetching data asynchronously and uses the async and await keywords to make the code more readable. The then method is used to handle the completion of the asynchronous operation.

An Extensive Standard Library

Dart includes a comprehensive standard library that provides a wide range of built-in classes and functions for common programming tasks. Whether you need to work with collections, manipulate strings, perform I/O operations, or interact with the web, Dart's standard library has you covered.

DartPad: An Interactive Playground

To get hands-on experience with Dart without installing any development tools, you can use DartPad, an online code editor and playground for Dart programming. It allows you to write, run, and experiment with Dart code directly in your web browser.

In summary, Dart is a versatile and modern programming language that serves as the foundation for Flutter's cross-platform capabilities. Its simple syntax, strong typing, object-oriented nature, and support for asynchronous programming make it well-suited for building high-performance and scalable applications. As you delve deeper into Flutter development, understanding Dart will be essential for crafting efficient and elegant code.

1.4. The Synergy of Flutter and Dart

Flutter and Dart, when combined, create a powerful synergy that enables developers to build cross-platform applications with exceptional performance and a stunning user interface. In this section, we'll explore how Flutter and Dart work together seamlessly to deliver a modern and efficient development experience.

Flutter's Use of Dart

Flutter is built on the Dart programming language, making it the primary language for developing Flutter applications. Dart's features and capabilities are harnessed by Flutter to achieve its goals of enabling cross-platform development, delivering a native-like experience, and optimizing performance.

One of the key reasons for using Dart as the foundation of Flutter is its efficiency and speed. Dart is a compiled language, which means that Dart code is transformed into native machine code during compilation. This results in faster execution and improved performance, ensuring that Flutter apps feel responsive and smooth.

Widget-Based UI Development

Flutter introduces a unique approach to user interface (UI) development, based on a tree of widgets. In Flutter, everything is a widget, from basic elements like buttons and text to complex layouts and even the entire application itself. This widget-based approach offers several advantages:

- **Reusability**: Widgets can be reused across different parts of the application, improving code maintainability and reducing duplication.
- **Customization**: Flutter widgets are highly customizable, allowing developers to achieve the desired look and feel for their applications.
- **Consistency**: Widgets ensure a consistent user interface, as they follow the same design and behavior principles across platforms.
- **Composability**: Widgets can be combined and nested to create complex UIs, providing flexibility in designing application layouts.

```
class MyApp extends StatelessWidget {
@override
Widget build(BuildContext context) {
return MaterialApp(
home: Scaffold(
appBar: AppBar(
title: Text('My Flutter App'),
),
```

```
body: Center(
child: Text('Hello, Flutter!'),
),
),
);
}
}
```

In this code snippet, we define a simple Flutter application using widgets. The MyApp widget serves as the root of the application, and it contains other widgets like MaterialApp, Scaffold, AppBar, and Text, which are assembled to create the final UI.

Dart's Role in the UI

Dart plays a crucial role in defining the structure and logic of Flutter applications. It is used to create and configure widgets, manage state, handle user interactions, and perform various computations. Dart's simplicity and expressiveness make it well-suited for defining the UI and the behavior of Flutter apps.

```
// Dart code defining a custom widget
class MyCustomWidget extends StatelessWidget {
final String text;
MyCustomWidget(this.text);
@override
Widget build(BuildContext context) {
```

```
return Container(
child: Text(
text,
style: TextStyle(fontSize: 18),
),
);
}
}
```

In this example, Dart code defines a custom widget called MyCustomWidget. The widget takes a text parameter and displays it within a Text widget, allowing for customization of the displayed text.

State Management in Dart

Dart is also responsible for managing the state of Flutter applications. State management is crucial for handling dynamic data, user input, and UI updates. Flutter offers various state management solutions, and Dart provides the necessary tools and language features to implement them effectively.

One popular state management solution in Flutter is the Provider package, which leverages Dart's capabilities for managing and providing data to widgets. With Provider, developers can efficiently manage the state of their applications and update the UI when data changes.

```
// Dart code using Provider for state management
```

```
final counterProvider = StateProvider<int>((ref) => 0);

class MyWidget extends ConsumerWidget {

@override

Widget build(BuildContext context, ScopedReader watch) {

final count = watch(counterProvider).state;

return Text('Count: $count');

}

}
```

In this Dart code snippet, we define a state provider using Provider, and the MyWidget widget uses the counterProvider to display the current count. Dart's language features, such as generics and closures, make it easy to work with state management solutions like Provider.

Conclusion

The synergy between Flutter and Dart is at the core of Flutter's success as a cross-platform UI toolkit. Dart's speed, simplicity, and versatility combined with Flutter's widget-based UI development and state management capabilities result in a powerful and efficient development platform. As you dive deeper into Flutter development, you'll discover how this synergy empowers you to create high-quality, visually appealing applications that run seamlessly on various platforms.

1.5. Setting Up Your Development Environment

Before you can start building Flutter applications with Dart, you need to set up your development environment. In this section, we'll walk through the steps to prepare your system for Flutter and Dart development.

Installing Flutter

1. **Download Flutter**: Visit the official Flutter website (https://flutter.dev) and download the Flutter SDK for your operating system. Flutter is available for Windows, macOS, and Linux.
2. **Extract the SDK**: Once downloaded, extract the Flutter SDK to a location on your computer.
3. **Add Flutter to PATH (Optional)**: To use Flutter commands globally from the terminal, you can add the Flutter binary directory to your system's PATH. This step is optional but recommended for a more convenient development experience.

```
export PATH="$PATH:`pwd`/flutter/bin"
```

1. **Initialize Flutter**: Open a terminal window and run the following command to initialize Flutter and set up the necessary dependencies:

```
flutter doctor
```

This command checks your system for any missing dependencies and provides recommendations on how to resolve them.

Installing Dart

1. **Download Dart SDK**: Dart is bundled with Flutter, so there is no need to download it separately. Installing Flutter, as mentioned earlier, will also provide you with the Dart SDK.
2. **Verify Dart Installation**: To verify that Dart is correctly installed along with Flutter, you can run the following command:

dart—version

This should display the Dart SDK version that matches the Flutter version you installed.

Integrated Development Environments (IDEs)

While you can develop Flutter and Dart applications using a plain text editor, using an Integrated Development Environment (IDE) can significantly enhance your productivity. Here are some popular IDEs for Flutter and Dart:

- **Visual Studio Code (VS Code)**: VS Code is a lightweight, open-source code editor developed by Microsoft. It has excellent support for Flutter and Dart development, including extensions and debugging tools.

- **Android Studio**: Android Studio is a powerful IDE for Android development that also includes robust support for Flutter and Dart. It provides a more integrated development experience if you're targeting Android devices.

- **IntelliJ IDEA**: IntelliJ IDEA, along with the Flutter and Dart plugins, offers a feature-rich development environment for building Flutter applications.

Choose the IDE that best suits your preferences and needs. Regardless of the IDE you choose, you'll need to install the Flutter and Dart plugins/extensions to enable Flutter development support.

Creating Your First Flutter Project

Now that you have Flutter and Dart set up, it's time to create your first Flutter project:

1. **Open Your IDE**: Launch your preferred IDE (VS Code, Android Studio, or IntelliJ IDEA) and ensure that the Flutter and Dart extensions/plugins are installed and enabled.
2. **Create a New Flutter Project**: Use the IDE's built-in tools to create a new Flutter project. You can typically do this by selecting "New Project" or "New Flutter Project" from the IDE's menu.
3. **Configure Project Settings**: Follow the prompts to configure your project settings, including choosing a project name, target platforms (iOS, Android, web, etc.), and other preferences.
4. **Run Your App**: Once your project is created, you can run your Flutter app on an emulator or physical device. Most IDEs provide a "Run" or "Debug" button to start your app.

```
void main() {

runApp(MyApp());

}
```

```
class MyApp extends StatelessWidget {
@override
Widget build(BuildContext context) {
return MaterialApp(
home: Scaffold(
appBar: AppBar(
title: Text('My First Flutter App'),
),
body: Center(
child: Text('Hello, Flutter!'),
),
),
);
}
}
```

This is a simple example of a Flutter app's entry point and UI. You can modify and expand upon this template as you learn more about Flutter and Dart.

With your development environment set up and your first Flutter project created, you're ready to start exploring the world of cross-platform app development with Flutter and Dart.

Chapter 2: Dart Basics

2.1. Syntax and Structure: Understanding Dart

Dart is a language known for its clear and concise syntax. Whether you're new to programming or transitioning from another language, understanding Dart's syntax and structure is crucial for effective development. In this section, we'll explore the fundamental elements of Dart, from variables to control flow, and provide examples to help you grasp the concepts.

Dart's Hello World

Let's start with a simple Dart program that prints "Hello, Dart!" to the console. In Dart, you use the main() function as the entry point for your program:

```
void main() {

print('Hello, Dart!');

}
```

- void main(): This is the main function that gets executed when you run your Dart program. The void keyword indicates that this function doesn't return a value.
- print('Hello, Dart!'): The print() function is used to output text to the console. In this case, it prints the string 'Hello, Dart!' followed by a newline.

Variables and Data Types

In Dart, you can declare variables using the var, final, or const keywords. Here are some examples:

var name = 'Alice'; // A variable that can change its value

final age = 30; // A variable that is read-only once assigned

const pi = 3.141592; // A compile-time constant

- var: Declares a variable that can change its value. Dart infers the variable's type based on the assigned value.

- final: Declares a read-only variable. Once assigned, its value cannot be changed.

- const: Declares a compile-time constant. These values are known at compile time and cannot change at runtime.

Dart has several built-in data types, including:

- int: Represents integer values, e.g., int age = 30;.

- double: Represents floating-point (decimal) values, e.g., double pi = 3.141592;.

- String: Represents a sequence of characters, e.g., String name = 'Alice';.

- bool: Represents a Boolean value (true or false), e.g., bool isFlutterAwesome = true;.

Control Flow: Loops and Conditionals

Dart supports common control flow structures, such as if statements and loops.

If Statements

```
if (age >= 18) {

print('You are an adult.');

} else {

print('You are a minor.');

}
```

The if statement checks the condition inside the parentheses and executes the code block within the curly braces if the condition is true. If the condition is false, the code inside the else block is executed.

Loops

Dart provides several types of loops, including for, while, and do-while. Here's an example of a for loop:

```
for (int i = 0; i < 5; i++) {

print('Iteration $i');

}
```

This for loop initializes a variable i to 0 and increments it with each iteration until it reaches 5. It prints the iteration number in each step.

Functions and Scope

Functions are essential in Dart for encapsulating reusable code blocks. Here's how you declare and call a function:

```
// Function declaration

int add(int a, int b) {

return a + b;

}

void main() {

// Function call

var result = add(3, 4);

print('The sum is $result');

}
```

- int add(int a, int b): This declares a function named add that takes two integer parameters a and b and returns their sum as an integer.
- void main(): The main function, as mentioned earlier, serves as the entry point of your Dart program.

Dart also has scope rules that determine where variables are accessible. Variables declared within a function are usually only accessible within that function, which is known as local scope. Variables declared outside of any function, like those declared in the main function, have a global scope and can be accessed throughout the program.

Comments

In Dart, you can add comments to your code using // for single-line comments and /* */ for multi-line comments:

// This is a single-line comment

/*

This is a multi-line comment.

It can span multiple lines.

*/

Comments are ignored by the Dart compiler and are solely for documentation and code readability.

Understanding these fundamental concepts of Dart's syntax and structure will provide you with a solid foundation for developing Flutter applications, where Dart serves as the primary programming language. As you progress, you'll explore more advanced topics and features of Dart that will enable you to create complex and feature-rich applications.

2.2. Variables, Types, and Operators

In Dart, variables are essential for storing and manipulating data. Understanding variable types and operators is crucial for effective programming. In this section, we'll delve into Dart's variable declarations, data types, and common operators.

Variable Declarations

Dart provides several ways to declare variables:

1. **Using var**: You can use the var keyword to declare variables with inferred types. Dart infers the type based on the assigned value.

var name = 'Alice'; // Inferred as String

var age = 30; // Inferred as int

1. **Using Explicit Types**: You can declare variables with explicit types using the type annotation:

String name = 'Alice';

int age = 30;

1. **Using final and const**: You can declare read-only variables using final and const. Once assigned, their values cannot change.

final String firstName = 'Alice';

const int legalAge = 18;

Data Types

Dart has a rich set of built-in data types:

1. **Numbers**: Dart supports integers and floating-point numbers.

– int: Represents integers (e.g., int age = 30;).

– double: Represents floating-point numbers (e.g., double pi = 3.141592;).

1. **Strings**: Dart uses the String type to represent text.

```
String name = 'Alice';
```

1. **Booleans**: Dart has a bool type for Boolean values, which can be either true or false.

```
bool isFlutterAwesome = true;
```

1. **Lists**: Lists are ordered collections of items.

```
List<int> numbers = [1, 2, 3];
```

1. **Maps**: Maps are key-value pairs.

```
Map<String, int> scores = {'Alice': 95, 'Bob': 88};
```

1. **Runes**: Dart supports Unicode characters and runes.

```
String chinese = '��';

Runes runes = chinese.runes;
```

1. **Symbols**: Symbols are used to represent identifiers at runtime.

```
Symbol mySymbol = #example;
```

Type Conversion

You can convert data between different types in Dart. Dart provides the following conversion methods:

- toString(): Converts a value to a string.

```
int age = 30;

String ageString = age.toString(); // Converts int to String
```

- int.parse(): Parses a string and converts it to an integer.

```
String ageString = '30';

int age = int.parse(ageString); // Converts String to int
```

- double.parse(): Parses a string and converts it to a double.

```
String piString = '3.141592';

double pi = double.parse(piString); // Converts String to double
```

Operators

Dart supports a variety of operators for performing operations on variables and values. Here are some common operators:

- **Arithmetic Operators**: Used for basic math operations.

```
int a = 10;

int b = 5;

int sum = a + b; // Addition

int difference = a - b; // Subtraction

int product = a * b; // Multiplication

double quotient = a / b; // Division

int remainder = a % b; // Modulus
```

- **Comparison Operators**: Used to compare values.

```
int x = 10;
int y = 5;
bool isEqual = x == y; // Equal to
bool isNotEqual = x != y; // Not equal to
bool isGreater = x > y; // Greater than
bool isLess = x < y; // Less than
bool isGreaterOrEqual = x >= y; // Greater than or equal to
bool isLessOrEqual = x <= y; // Less than or equal to
```

- **Logical Operators**: Used for logical operations.

```
bool isTrue = true;
bool isFalse = false;
bool andResult = isTrue && isFalse; // Logical AND
bool orResult = isTrue || isFalse; // Logical OR
bool notResult = !isTrue; // Logical NOT
```

- **Assignment Operators**: Used to assign values.

```
int num = 10;
num += 5; // Equivalent to num = num + 5
num -= 3; // Equivalent to num = num - 3
```

- **Conditional Operator (Ternary)**: A concise way to express conditional statements.

```
bool isAdult = age >= 18 ? true : false;
```

Understanding variables, data types, and operators is fundamental to programming in Dart. These concepts form the building blocks for more complex code and logic as you continue to develop Dart and Flutter applications.

2.3. Control Flow: Loops and Conditionals

Control flow structures in Dart, such as loops and conditionals, allow you to make decisions, repeat actions, and create more complex logic in your programs. In this section, we'll explore the various control flow statements available in Dart.

Conditional Statements

Conditional statements allow you to execute different blocks of code based on specified conditions. The primary conditional statement in Dart is the if statement.

if Statement

The if statement evaluates a condition and executes a block of code if the condition is true. Here's a basic example:

```
bool isRaining = true;

if (isRaining) {

print('Bring an umbrella.');

}
```

In this example, the message "Bring an umbrella." will be printed to the console only if the isRaining variable is true.

if-else Statement

You can also use the if-else statement to specify an alternative block of code to execute if the condition is false:

```
int age = 20;

if (age >= 18) {

print('You are an adult.');

} else {

print('You are a minor.');

}
```

In this case, if the age is greater than or equal to 18, it prints "You are an adult."; otherwise, it prints "You are a minor."

if-else if-else Statement

For multiple conditions, you can use the if-else if-else statement:

```
int score = 85;

if (score >= 90) {

print('A');

} else if (score >= 80) {

print('B');
```

```
} else if (score >= 70) {

print('C');

} else {

print('F');

}
```

This example assigns letter grades based on the score variable.

Loops

Loops in Dart allow you to repeat a block of code multiple times, making it easier to work with collections or perform repetitive tasks.

for Loop

The for loop is used to iterate over a sequence of values. Here's a simple example:

```
for (int i = 0; i < 5; i++) {

print('Iteration $i');

}
```

This for loop will print "Iteration 0" through "Iteration 4" to the console.

while Loop

The while loop repeatedly executes a block of code while a condition is true. Here's an example:

```
int count = 0;
```

```
while (count < 3) {

print('Count: $count');

count++;

}
```

This while loop will print "Count: 0", "Count: 1", and "Count: 2" to the console.

do-while Loop

The do-while loop is similar to the while loop, but it guarantees that the block of code is executed at least once, even if the condition is false:

```
int x = 0;

do {

print('Value of x: $x');

x++;

} while (x < 3);
```

This do-while loop will also print "Value of x: 0", "Value of x: 1", and "Value of x: 2" to the console.

Control Flow with break and continue

In addition to the basic control flow statements, Dart provides the break and continue statements to further control the flow of your program.

- The break statement is used to exit a loop prematurely. It can be used in for, while, and do-while loops.

```
for (int i = 0; i < 5; i++) {

if (i == 3) {

break; // Exit the loop when i is 3

}

print('Iteration $i');

}
```

- The continue statement is used to skip the rest of the current iteration and proceed to the next iteration of a loop.

```
for (int i = 0; i < 5; i++) {

if (i == 3) {

continue; // Skip iteration when i is 3

}

print('Iteration $i');

}
```

Understanding conditional statements and loops is fundamental for building programs that can make decisions and perform repetitive tasks. These control flow structures are essential building blocks for more complex Dart applications and are frequently used in conjunction with variables and functions to create sophisticated logic.

2.4. Functions and Scope

Functions are a fundamental concept in Dart, allowing you to encapsulate blocks of code for reuse and modularity. In this section, we'll explore how to declare, define, and use functions in Dart, along with the concept of variable scope.

Declaring Functions

In Dart, you declare a function using the functionName(parameters) syntax. Here's a basic example of a function:

```
// Function declaration

void greet() {

print('Hello, Dart!');

}
```

In this example, we declare a function named greet that doesn't take any parameters and doesn't return a value (void). The function prints "Hello, Dart!" when called.

Function Parameters

Functions can take parameters, which allow you to pass data into the function. Here's an example with parameters:

```
// Function declaration with parameters

void greetPerson(String name) {

print('Hello, $name!');

}
```

In this example, the greetPerson function takes a single parameter name, which is a String. When called, you provide an argument for the name parameter, and the function uses it to print a personalized greeting.

Returning Values

Functions can also return values using the return keyword. Here's an example:

```
// Function declaration with a return value

int add(int a, int b) {

return a + b;

}
```

In this example, the add function takes two integer parameters (a and b) and returns their sum as an integer. You can store the result of the function call in a variable or use it directly.

```
int result = add(3, 4); // result is 7
```

Optional Parameters

In Dart, you can declare optional parameters by wrapping them in square brackets []. This allows you to call a function with or without providing values for those parameters.

```
// Function declaration with optional parameters

void printDetails(String name, [int age = 0]) {

print('Name: $name');

if (age != 0) {
```

```
print('Age: $age');

}

}
```

In this example, the printDetails function takes a required parameter name and an optional parameter age. If age is not provided when calling the function, it defaults to 0. You can call the function with or without specifying the age argument.

```
printDetails('Alice'); // Only name is provided

printDetails('Bob', 30); // Both name and age are provided
```

Named Parameters

Named parameters allow you to specify parameters by name when calling a function, regardless of their order. You declare named parameters using curly braces {} in the function signature.

```
// Function declaration with named parameters

void greet({String name = 'Dart', String message = 'Hello'}) {

print('$message, $name!');

}
```

In this example, the greet function takes two named parameters (name and message) with default values. When calling the function, you can specify the parameters by name:

```
greet(name: 'Alice'); // Output: Hello, Alice!

greet(message: 'Hi', name: 'Bob'); // Output: Hi, Bob!
```

Function Scope

Dart follows a scoping mechanism, meaning that variables declared within a function are typically only accessible within that function. This is known as local scope. Variables declared outside of any function have global scope and can be accessed throughout the program.

```
int globalVariable = 10; // Global variable

void printValues() {

int localVariable = 20; // Local variable

print('Global: $globalVariable, Local: $localVariable');

}

void main() {

printValues();

// Accessing the global variable is possible here

// Local variable is not accessible here

}
```

In this example, globalVariable is accessible within both the printValues function and the main function, while localVariable is only accessible within the printValues function.

Understanding how to declare and use functions, pass parameters, and handle scope is crucial for creating organized and modular Dart code. Functions help you structure your code logically, promote code reuse, and make your programs more maintainable and readable.

2.5. Classes and Objects in Dart

Classes and objects are fundamental concepts in object-oriented programming (OOP) languages like Dart. In this section, we'll explore how to create classes, define objects, and work with OOP principles in Dart.

Creating Classes

A class is a blueprint for creating objects. It defines the properties (attributes) and behaviors (methods) that objects of the class will have. To create a class in Dart, you use the class keyword followed by the class name. Here's a simple example:

```
// Class declaration

class Person {

// Properties or fields

String name;

int age;

// Constructor

Person(String name, int age) {

this.name = name;

this.age = age;

}

// Method

void sayHello() {
```

```
print('Hello, my name is $name, and I am $age years old.');
}
}
```

In this example, we define a Person class with two properties (name and age) and a method (sayHello). The constructor is a special method used for initializing objects when they are created.

Creating Objects

Once you have defined a class, you can create objects (instances) of that class using the new keyword or simply by calling the constructor. Here's how you create a Person object:

```
// Creating objects
Person alice = Person('Alice', 30);
Person bob = Person('Bob', 25);
```

In this code, we create two Person objects, alice and bob, by calling the Person constructor with the respective values for name and age.

Accessing Properties and Methods

You can access the properties and methods of an object using the dot (.) notation. For example:

```
print(alice.name); // Accessing the 'name' property
print(bob.age); // Accessing the 'age' property
alice.sayHello(); // Calling the 'sayHello' method for 'alice'
bob.sayHello(); // Calling the 'sayHello' method for 'bob'
```

In this code, we access the properties (name and age) and call the sayHello method on the alice and bob objects.

Constructors

Constructors are special methods used to initialize objects. In Dart, you can have multiple constructors, including named constructors. Here's an example of a class with multiple constructors:

```
class Student {

String name;

int age;

// Default constructor

Student(this.name, this.age);

// Named constructor

Student.withDefaultAge(String name) {

this.name = name;

this.age = 18; // Default age

}

}
```

In this Student class, we have a default constructor that takes name and age as parameters and a named constructor Student.withDefaultAge that only takes name as a parameter and sets a default age of 18.

Getters and Setters

Dart allows you to create getter and setter methods to control access to class properties. Getters are used to retrieve property values, and setters are used to change them. Here's an example:

```
class Temperature {

double _celsius = 0; // Private property

// Getter

double get celsius => _celsius;

// Setter

set celsius(double value) {

if (value >= -273.15) {

_celsius = value;

}

}

}
```

In this Temperature class, we have a private property _celsius, a getter celsius to retrieve its value, and a setter celsius to set its value. The setter includes a validation check to ensure the temperature is not below absolute zero.

Inheritance

Dart supports inheritance, allowing you to create new classes based on existing ones. The extends keyword is used to inherit from a parent class. Here's an example:

```
class Animal {
String name;
Animal(this.name);
void speak() {
print('$name makes a sound');
}
}
class Dog extends Animal {
Dog(String name) : super(name);
@override
void speak() {
print('$name barks');
}
}
```

In this code, we have an Animal class with a speak method, and a Dog class that extends Animal. The Dog class overrides the speak method to provide a specific implementation for dogs.

Abstract Classes

Dart also supports abstract classes, which are classes that cannot be instantiated directly but can be used as a blueprint for other classes. To define an abstract class, use the abstract keyword:

```
abstract class Shape {
```

```
double calculateArea();
}
```

In this example, the Shape class is abstract and includes an abstract method calculateArea(). Subclasses that inherit from Shape are required to provide an implementation for calculateArea().

Understanding classes and objects is a fundamental aspect of Dart programming and object-oriented programming in general. Classes allow you to model real-world entities, encapsulate data and behavior, and create modular and maintainable code. Whether you're building Flutter applications or other Dart projects, knowing how to work with classes and objects is essential.

Chapter 3: Flutter Fundamentals

3.1. Understanding Widgets and Their Importance

In Flutter, everything is a widget. Widgets are the building blocks of your user interface (UI) and are responsible for rendering the visual elements of your app. Understanding widgets and their importance is crucial when working with Flutter.

What Are Widgets?

Widgets are UI components that can be as simple as a button or as complex as an entire screen. Flutter provides a rich library of pre-built widgets, and you can also create your own custom widgets.

Widgets can be categorized into two main types:

1. **Stateless Widgets**: These are widgets that do not have any mutable state. They are purely based on their configuration and can be thought of as "immutable" components. Stateless widgets are ideal for parts of the UI that do not change once rendered.
2. **Stateful Widgets**: These are widgets that have mutable state. They can change and rebuild themselves based on that state. Stateful widgets are used for parts of the UI that need to update dynamically in response to user interactions or other events.

The Widget Tree

In a Flutter app, the UI is represented as a hierarchy of widgets known as the "widget tree." At the root of the widget tree is typically a MaterialApp or CupertinoApp widget, depending on whether you are building a Material Design or iOS-style app. These top-level widgets serve as the entry points for your app.

The widget tree is composed of parent and child widgets, forming a tree structure. Parent widgets can contain one or more child widgets, and child widgets can, in turn, be parents to other widgets. This hierarchical arrangement allows you to compose complex UIs by combining smaller, reusable widgets.

Building UIs with Composition

One of the key concepts in Flutter is the idea of composing UIs by combining widgets. You can create custom UI components by nesting and arranging widgets in a hierarchy. For example, you can build a user profile card using a combination of widgets like Container, Image, Text, and IconButton. Each of these widgets is responsible for rendering a specific part of the card.

Here's a simple example of a stateless widget that displays a user profile card:

```
class UserProfileCard extends StatelessWidget {

final String name;

final String imageUrl;

UserProfileCard({required this.name, required this.imageUrl});

@override

Widget build(BuildContext context) {

return Card(

elevation: 3,
```

```
child: Column(
children: [
Image.network(imageUrl),
Padding(
padding: EdgeInsets.all(16),
child: Text(
name,
style: TextStyle(fontSize: 18, fontWeight: FontWeight.bold),
),
),
IconButton(
icon: Icon(Icons.favorite),
onPressed: () {
// Handle favorite button tap
},
),
],
),
);
}
```

```
}
```

In this example, the UserProfileCard widget is composed of several other widgets, including Card, Image, Text, and IconButton. These widgets work together to create a cohesive user interface.

Hot Reload and Rapid Iteration

One of the advantages of Flutter is its hot reload feature, which allows you to make changes to your code and see the results almost instantly without restarting the app. This rapid iteration cycle speeds up development and makes it easy to experiment with different UI layouts and styles.

Conclusion

Widgets are the fundamental building blocks of a Flutter app's user interface. Understanding how to use widgets to compose UIs is essential for creating visually appealing and interactive mobile applications. In the next sections, we will delve deeper into the concepts of stateless and stateful widgets, layouts, navigation, and user input handling, building on the foundation of widget-based development.

3.2. State Management: Stateless and Stateful Widgets

State management is a fundamental concept in Flutter, and it revolves around the idea of handling the mutable data and behavior of your app's UI. In this section, we'll explore stateless and stateful widgets and how they play a crucial role in managing the state of your Flutter application.

Stateless Widgets

Stateless widgets, as the name suggests, are widgets that do not have any mutable state. Once created, they remain the same until they are destroyed or removed from the widget tree. Stateless widgets are primarily used for parts of the UI that do not change once rendered.

Here's a simple example of a stateless widget:

```
class MyStatelessWidget extends StatelessWidget {

@override

Widget build(BuildContext context) {

return Container(

color: Colors.blue,

child: Text('This is a stateless widget'),

);

}

}
```

In this example, MyStatelessWidget is a stateless widget that renders a blue container with text. The content of this widget is fixed and cannot change after it's built.

Stateful Widgets

Stateful widgets, on the other hand, have mutable state and can change their appearance or behavior in response to events, user interactions, or data updates. Stateful widgets are used for parts of the UI that need to update dynamically.

To create a stateful widget, you typically pair it with a separate mutable object called a "state" object. The state object is responsible for holding and managing the mutable data for the widget.

Here's an example of a stateful widget:

```
class MyStatefulWidget extends StatefulWidget {

@override

_MyStatefulWidgetState createState() =>
_MyStatefulWidgetState();

}

class _MyStatefulWidgetState extends State<MyStatefulWidget> {

int _counter = 0;

void _incrementCounter() {

setState(() {

_counter++;

});

}

@override

Widget build(BuildContext context) {

return Column(

children: [

Text('Counter: $_counter'),
```

```
ElevatedButton(
onPressed: _incrementCounter,
child: Text('Increment'),
),
],
);
}
}
```

In this example, MyStatefulWidget is a stateful widget paired with _MyStatefulWidgetState, which is the state object. The state object contains a mutable variable _counter that tracks the number of times a button is pressed. When the button is pressed, the _incrementCounter function is called to update the state using setState(), triggering a rebuild of the widget with the updated data.

Choosing Between Stateless and Stateful Widgets

When deciding whether to use a stateless or stateful widget, consider the following guidelines:

- Use stateless widgets for parts of the UI that do not change over time, such as static text or images.
- Use stateful widgets when you need to manage mutable data, respond to user interactions, or update the UI dynamically.
- If a widget depends on external data or user input, it's likely a candidate for a stateful widget.

- Be mindful of performance considerations when using stateful widgets, as frequent rebuilds can impact app performance. Use tools like the Flutter DevTools to analyze performance bottlenecks.

Understanding how to use stateless and stateful widgets is crucial for effective state management in Flutter. These widgets serve as the foundation for building dynamic and interactive user interfaces in your Flutter applications. In the following sections, we'll delve deeper into state management techniques, including using providers, the BLoC pattern, and Redux.

3.3. Layouts and UI Components

Layouts and UI components are essential parts of any Flutter app, as they define how the user interface is structured and how various elements are displayed on the screen. In this section, we'll explore the concepts of layouts and UI components in Flutter.

Layouts

Layouts in Flutter determine the arrangement and positioning of widgets within your app's UI. Flutter offers a variety of layout widgets that allow you to create flexible and responsive user interfaces. Some of the commonly used layout widgets include:

- **Container**: A versatile widget that can contain other widgets and allows you to set properties like padding, margin, and color.

- **Row and Column**: Used to create horizontal and vertical layouts, respectively, by arranging child widgets in a row or column.

- **ListView**: A scrollable list of widgets that can be used to display a large number of items.

- **Stack**: Allows you to layer widgets on top of each other, enabling complex layouts and overlapping elements.

- **Expanded**: A widget that expands to fill available space within its parent, typically used within rows and columns to control widget sizing.

- **GridView**: Used to create a grid of widgets, making it suitable for displaying items in a grid pattern.

Here's a simple example of using the Row and Column layout widgets:

```
Column(

children: [

Text('First item'),

Text('Second item'),

Text('Third item'),

],

)
```

In this code, we create a vertical column with three text widgets, resulting in a vertically stacked list of items.

UI Components

UI components in Flutter are widgets that represent visual elements such as buttons, images, text, and more. Flutter provides a wide range of pre-built UI components that you can use in your app. Some commonly used UI components include:

- **Text**: Used for displaying textual content with various styling options.
- **Image**: Displays images from various sources, including assets, URLs, and local files.
- **Button**: Represents interactive buttons that users can tap on.
- **TextField**: Provides a text input field for users to enter text.
- **Icon**: Renders icons and symbols from a built-in icon library.
- **Card**: A material design card that can contain other widgets, commonly used for displaying information in a structured format.
- **AppBar**: A top app bar typically used for app navigation and screen titles.

Here's an example of using the Text and Button UI components:

```
Column(
children: [
Text('Welcome to Flutter!'),
ElevatedButton(
onPressed: () {
```

```
// Handle button press
},
child: Text('Get Started'),
),
],
)
```

In this code, we create a column containing a text widget and a button widget. The button widget is interactive and triggers an action when pressed.

Custom UI Components

While Flutter provides a rich set of built-in UI components, you can also create custom UI components by composing widgets together. Custom UI components allow you to design unique and tailored user interfaces that match your app's requirements.

For example, you can create a custom button with a specific design and behavior by combining various widgets like Container, Text, and GestureDetector. Custom UI components give you full control over the appearance and functionality of your app's elements.

Understanding layouts and UI components is crucial for designing and building user-friendly and visually appealing Flutter apps. The choice of layouts and the use of appropriate UI components play a significant role in creating an intuitive and engaging user experience. In the following sections, we'll explore navigation between screens, handling user input, and styling and theming your app to enhance its overall design and functionality.

3.4. Navigating Between Screens

In Flutter app development, navigating between different screens or pages is a common requirement. Flutter provides a powerful navigation system that allows you to move between various parts of your app's user interface seamlessly. In this section, we'll explore how to implement navigation in Flutter.

The Navigator Widget

Flutter's navigation system is built around the Navigator widget, which manages a stack of "routes." Each route represents a distinct screen or page in your app. You can push new routes onto the stack to navigate forward and pop routes to go back.

Here's an overview of how navigation works with the Navigator widget:

- **Pushing Routes**: To navigate to a new screen, you push a new route onto the navigator's stack. This can be achieved using the Navigator.push() method. The new route typically represents the screen you want to navigate to and may include a widget as its content.

- **Popping Routes**: To go back to the previous screen, you pop the current route from the navigator's stack. This can be done using the Navigator.pop() method. The top route is removed from the stack, and the screen reverts to the previous one.

Using MaterialPageRoute

One of the most common ways to implement navigation in Flutter is by using the MaterialPageRoute class. This class provides a convenient way to create and manage routes that adhere to the Material Design guidelines.

Here's an example of how to navigate to a new screen using MaterialPageRoute:

```
ElevatedButton(

onPressed: () {

Navigator.push(

context,

MaterialPageRoute(builder: (context) => SecondScreen()),

);

},

child: Text('Go to Second Screen'),

)
```

In this code, we use the Navigator.push() method to push a new route onto the navigator's stack. The builder function defines the content of the new route, which is represented by the SecondScreen widget. When the button is pressed, the app navigates to the SecondScreen.

Passing Data between Screens

Often, you'll need to pass data from one screen to another when navigating. Flutter provides a way to pass data as arguments when pushing a new route. Here's an example:

```
ElevatedButton(
```

```
onPressed: () {
Navigator.push(
context,
MaterialPageRoute(
builder: (context) => SecondScreen(data: 'Hello from First Screen!'),
),
);
},
child: Text('Go to Second Screen with Data'),
)
```

In this code, we pass a string 'Hello from First Screen!' as data to the SecondScreen. Inside SecondScreen, you can access this data through the constructor and use it as needed.

Named Routes

While using MaterialPageRoute is straightforward, Flutter also supports named routes. Named routes allow you to define routes with meaningful names and navigate between them using those names. This can make your code more organized, especially in larger apps.

To define named routes, you typically provide a Map of route names to builder functions in your app's MaterialApp:

```
MaterialApp(
```

```
routes: {
'/': (context) => HomeScreen(),
'/second': (context) => SecondScreen(),
'/third': (context) => ThirdScreen(),
},
// ...
)
```

With named routes defined, you can navigate to a specific route using the Navigator.pushNamed() method:

```
ElevatedButton(
onPressed: () {
Navigator.pushNamed(context, '/second');
},
child: Text('Go to Second Screen'),
)
```

Handling Navigation Back

To handle going back to the previous screen, you can use the Navigator.pop() method. For example, if you have a button on the second screen to navigate back to the first screen:

```
ElevatedButton(
onPressed: () {
```

```
Navigator.pop(context);
},
child: Text('Back to First Screen'),
)
```

This code pops the top route from the stack, returning to the previous screen.

Conclusion

Implementing navigation between screens is a fundamental aspect of building Flutter apps. Flutter's Navigator widget and MaterialPageRoute class provide powerful tools for managing the navigation flow within your app. Whether you choose to use named routes or push routes dynamically, understanding how to navigate between screens is essential for creating a seamless user experience. In the following sections, we'll explore handling user input, performing network requests, and managing state in Flutter apps.

3.5. Handling User Input and Forms

User input is a fundamental aspect of most mobile applications, allowing users to interact with your app's functionality. Flutter provides various widgets and techniques for handling user input and forms effectively. In this section, we'll explore how to capture user input and manage forms in Flutter.

Basic User Input

Flutter offers a range of widgets for capturing basic user input. Some of the commonly used widgets include:

- **TextField**: A widget for capturing text input, such as user names, passwords, and search queries.
- **Checkbox**: Allows users to toggle a binary choice, such as a yes/no decision.
- **Radio**: Used for selecting a single option from a group of choices.
- **Switch**: Provides an on/off toggle switch for options.
- **Slider**: Allows users to select a value within a specified range by sliding a thumb along a track.
- **DropdownButton**: Presents users with a list of choices in a dropdown menu.

Here's an example of a TextField widget for capturing text input:

```
TextField(
onChanged: (value) {
// Handle text input changes
},
decoration: InputDecoration(
labelText: 'Enter your name',
),
)
```

In this code, the TextField widget captures text input and provides an onChanged callback to handle changes to the input. The

InputDecoration allows you to customize the appearance of the input field.

Form Widgets

When working with forms that consist of multiple input fields, Flutter provides the Form widget, along with related widgets such as TextFormField, CheckboxListTile, and RadioListTile. The Form widget helps you manage the state of form fields, validate user input, and submit form data.

Here's an example of a simple form with two text fields:

```
final _formKey = GlobalKey<FormState>();

@override

Widget build(BuildContext context) {

return Form(

key: _formKey,

child: Column(

children: [

TextFormField(

validator: (value) {

if (value == null || value.isEmpty) {

return 'Please enter your name';

}

return null;
```

```
},
decoration: InputDecoration(
labelText: 'Name',
),
),
TextFormField(
validator: (value) {
if (value == null || value.isEmpty) {
return 'Please enter your email';
}
return null;
},
decoration: InputDecoration(
labelText: 'Email',
),
),
ElevatedButton(
onPressed: () {
if (_formKey.currentState!.validate()) {
// Form is valid, submit data
```

```
}
},
child: Text('Submit'),
),
],
),
);
}
```

In this code, we define a Form widget with two TextFormField widgets for capturing the user's name and email. The validator property is used to validate the input fields, and the ElevatedButton triggers form submission if the form is valid.

Handling User Interactions

In addition to capturing text input, Flutter allows you to handle various user interactions, such as button taps and gestures. For example, you can use the GestureDetector widget to detect taps, swipes, and other gestures.

Here's an example of using GestureDetector to detect a tap gesture:

```
GestureDetector(
onTap: () {
// Handle tap gesture
},
```

```
child: Container(
color: Colors.blue,
child: Center(
child: Text('Tap me!'),
),
),
)
```

In this code, the GestureDetector wraps a Container with a text label. When the user taps on the container, the onTap callback is triggered, allowing you to respond to the tap gesture.

Complex User Interfaces

For more complex user interfaces that require custom interactions, you can use the GestureDetector and Listener widgets to capture various gestures and events. Additionally, Flutter offers plugins and libraries for handling advanced input scenarios, such as capturing handwriting, scanning barcodes, or implementing complex gesture recognition.

Handling user input and forms effectively is crucial for creating user-friendly and interactive Flutter apps. Whether you need to capture simple text input or implement complex gesture-based interactions, Flutter provides a range of widgets and tools to meet your requirements. In the following sections, we'll explore advanced topics such as state management, network requests, and building responsive and beautiful UIs.

Chapter 4: Advanced Dart Concepts

4.1. Asynchronous Programming with Futures and Streams

Asynchronous programming is a crucial aspect of modern app development, allowing applications to perform non-blocking operations such as network requests, file I/O, and more without freezing the user interface. Dart provides a robust and expressive model for handling asynchronous operations through the use of Futures and Streams. In this section, we will delve into the concepts of Futures and Streams and how they enable asynchronous programming in Dart.

Understanding Futures

A **Future** in Dart represents a potential value or error that will be available at some point in the future. Futures are used to perform asynchronous operations and handle their results. You can think of a Future as a placeholder for a value that will eventually be computed or fetched.

Here's a simple example of using a Future to simulate a delayed operation:

```
Future<int> fetchUserData() async {

await Future.delayed(Duration(seconds: 2)); // Simulate a 2-second delay

return 42; // Simulated user data

}
```

```
void main() async {

print('Fetching user data...');

final userData = await fetchUserData();

print('User data: $userData');

}
```

In this code, fetchUserData returns a Future that resolves to an integer (simulated user data) after a 2-second delay. The await keyword is used to wait for the Future to complete, allowing us to print the user data when it's available.

Handling Errors with Futures

Futures can represent successful values or errors. You can handle errors by using the catchError method or the try-catch block when working with Futures. Here's an example:

```
Future<void> fetchData() async {

try {

// Simulate a network request

await Future.delayed(Duration(seconds: 2));

throw Exception('Failed to fetch data');

} catch (error) {

print('Error: $error');

}

}
```

```
void main() async {
print('Fetching data...');
await fetchData();
print('Data fetched.');
}
```

In this example, the fetchData function simulates a network request and intentionally throws an error. We catch the error and handle it within the try-catch block.

Working with Streams

While Futures represent a single value or error that will be available in the future, **Streams** represent a sequence of values or events over time. Streams are used for handling continuous or asynchronous data, such as real-time updates, user input, or data streams from external sources.

Dart provides the Stream and StreamController classes to work with streams. Here's a simple example of a stream that emits values over time:

```
import 'dart:async';
void main() {
final streamController = StreamController<int>();
final subscription = streamController.stream.listen((value) {
print('Received: $value');
});
```

```
streamController.sink.add(1);

streamController.sink.add(2);

streamController.sink.add(3);

subscription.cancel();

streamController.close();

}
```

In this code, we create a StreamController to manage the stream and use the listen method to subscribe to the stream and receive values. We add values to the stream using the sink, and we cancel the subscription and close the stream when done.

Working with Async and Await

Dart's async and await keywords simplify working with asynchronous code, making it look more like synchronous code. You can use them with both Futures and Streams to await results or values without blocking the program's execution.

Here's an example of using async and await with a Future:

```
Future<int> fetchUserAge() async {

await Future.delayed(Duration(seconds: 2)); // Simulate a delay

return 30;

}

void main() async {

print('Fetching user age...');
```

```
final age = await fetchUserAge();

print('User age: $age');

}
```

In this code, we use async and await to wait for the fetchUserAge Future to complete and retrieve the user's age.

Conclusion

Asynchronous programming is a crucial skill for Dart developers, allowing applications to perform tasks efficiently without blocking the user interface. Dart's Futures and Streams provide powerful mechanisms for working with asynchronous operations, handling errors, and managing data streams over time. Understanding how to use Futures and Streams effectively is essential for developing responsive and efficient Dart and Flutter applications. In the following sections, we will explore more advanced Dart concepts, best practices, and techniques for developing robust applications.

4.2. Effective Dart: Best Practices

Effective Dart programming involves following a set of best practices and guidelines to write clean, maintainable, and efficient Dart code. These practices help ensure that your code is readable, robust, and easy to maintain, making it a valuable resource for both developers and future maintainers of your codebase. In this section, we'll explore some essential best practices for writing effective Dart code.

1. Code Formatting and Style

Consistent code formatting and style improve code readability and maintainability. Dart provides a tool called dartfmt that automatically formats your code according to the Dart style guide.

It's a good practice to run dartfmt on your code regularly to keep it consistent.

You can format your Dart code using the following command:

```
dart format .
```

2. Use Meaningful Variable and Function Names

Choose descriptive and meaningful names for variables, functions, classes, and other identifiers. This makes your code self-explanatory and easier to understand. Avoid using single-letter variable names (e.g., x, i) unless they have a clear and well-understood context.

```
// Good variable naming

int age = 30;

String username = 'john_doe';

// Avoid using single-letter variable names

int a = 30; // Not clear

String u = 'john_doe'; // Not clear
```

3. Follow the Dart Style Guide

Adhering to the official Dart Style Guide helps maintain a consistent coding style across your project. The style guide covers topics like indentation, naming conventions, and code structure. Following the guide makes your code more accessible to other Dart developers.

4. Avoid Mutability Where Possible

Immutability can lead to safer and more predictable code. Use the final keyword for variables that should not change after initialization. Immutable data structures and values can help prevent bugs related to unintended side effects.

```
// Use 'final' for immutable variables

final int age = 30;

final String username = 'john_doe';

// Avoid mutable variables if not needed

int mutableAge = 30;

String mutableUsername = 'john_doe';
```

5. Null Safety

Dart introduced null safety to help eliminate null pointer exceptions. It's a good practice to enable null safety for your Dart projects by adding the following to your pubspec.yaml file:

```
environment:

sdk: ">=2.12.0 <3.0.0"
```

Null safety encourages you to use non-nullable types and handle null values explicitly when needed.

6. Document Your Code

Use comments and documentation to explain the purpose and usage of your code. Dart supports both single-line and multi-line comments. Additionally, you can generate documentation using tools like dartdoc.

```
/// This function calculates the sum of two numbers.

int add(int a, int b) {
```

```
return a + b;

}

// Single-line comment

int subtract(int a, int b) {

return a - b;

}
```

7. Modularize Your Code

Break your code into smaller, reusable modules or packages. Well-structured code with clear separation of concerns is easier to maintain and test. Dart's package management system (Pub) makes it simple to create and distribute reusable packages.

8. Testing

Write unit tests for your Dart code to catch bugs early and ensure code reliability. The Dart testing framework provides tools for writing and running tests.

9. Error Handling

Handle exceptions gracefully by using try-catch blocks. Provide meaningful error messages and log errors appropriately. Avoid using generic catch clauses unless necessary.

```
try {

// Risky code here

} catch (e) {
```

```
print('An error occurred: $e');

}
```

10. Optimize for Performance

Profile your code to identify and optimize performance bottlenecks. Dart's tools, like the Observatory and Flutter DevTools, can help you analyze and optimize your code for better performance.

These best practices lay the foundation for writing clean, maintainable, and effective Dart code. Following them will lead to code that is easier to read, understand, and maintain, ultimately benefiting your project and team.

4.3. Generics and Collections

Generics and collections are powerful features in Dart that allow you to write code that is more flexible and type-safe. They enable you to work with different data types while maintaining compile-time type checking. In this section, we'll explore the concepts of generics and collections in Dart and how they can be used effectively in your code.

Generics

Generics in Dart enable you to write reusable code that can work with different data types while preserving type safety. They are often used in classes, functions, and methods to work with collections, such as lists, sets, and maps, in a type-safe manner.

Here's a simple example of a generic function that takes a list of any data type and returns its length:

```
int findLength<T>(List<T> list) {
```

```
return list.length;

}

void main() {

List<int> integers = [1, 2, 3, 4, 5];

List<String> strings = ['apple', 'banana', 'cherry'];

print('Length of integers: ${findLength<int>(integers)}');

print('Length of strings: ${findLength<String>(strings)}');

}
```

In this code, findLength is a generic function that can accept a list of any data type T. The type T is determined when the function is called. This allows you to use the function with different types of lists while ensuring type safety.

Collections

Dart provides a variety of collection classes that are highly efficient and flexible. Some of the most commonly used collection types include:

- **List**: An ordered collection of elements, often referred to as an array. Lists can contain duplicates, and their elements are indexed by integers.

- **Set**: An unordered collection of unique elements. Sets do not allow duplicate values.

- **Map**: A key-value pair collection where each key is associated with a value. Maps are also known as dictionaries or associative arrays.

Here's an example of using these collection types:

```
List<int> numbers = [1, 2, 3, 4, 5];

Set<String> fruits = {'apple', 'banana', 'cherry'};

Map<String, int> scores = {'Alice': 95, 'Bob': 88, 'Charlie': 92};

print(numbers[0]); // Accessing the first element of the list

print(fruits.contains('apple')); // Checking if 'apple' is in the set

print(scores['Bob']); // Accessing Bob's score in the map
```

Working with Collections

Dart provides a rich set of methods and operators for working with collections. For example, you can use the forEach method to iterate over the elements of a list, the add and remove methods to modify lists and sets, and the putIfAbsent method to update map entries.

```
List<int> numbers = [1, 2, 3, 4, 5];

// Iterating over the list

numbers.forEach((number) {

print(number);

});

Set<String> fruits = {'apple', 'banana', 'cherry'};

// Adding an element to the set

fruits.add('orange');

Map<String, int> scores = {'Alice': 95, 'Bob': 88, 'Charlie': 92};
```

```
// Updating a map entry or adding it if absent

scores.putIfAbsent('David', () => 78);
```

Collection Literals

Dart provides concise ways to create collection literals using square brackets [] for lists, curly braces {} for sets, and colons : for maps.

```
List<int> numbers = [1, 2, 3, 4, 5];

Set<String> fruits = {'apple', 'banana', 'cherry'};

Map<String, int> scores = {'Alice': 95, 'Bob': 88, 'Charlie': 92};
```

These collection literals make it easy to initialize and work with collections in Dart.

Conclusion

Generics and collections are fundamental concepts in Dart that empower you to write flexible and type-safe code. Generics allow you to create reusable functions and classes that work with different data types, while collections provide efficient data structures for storing and manipulating data. By mastering these concepts, you can write more efficient and maintainable Dart code for a wide range of applications.

4.4. Exception Handling and Debugging

Exception handling is an essential part of writing robust and reliable Dart code. It allows you to gracefully handle unexpected errors and failures that may occur during program execution. In this section, we'll explore exception handling techniques in Dart and how to effectively debug your Dart applications.

Handling Exceptions

In Dart, exceptions are objects that represent errors or unexpected conditions that may occur during runtime. Dart provides a built-in exception hierarchy, and you can create custom exceptions to suit your application's needs.

The try-catch Block

The most common way to handle exceptions in Dart is by using the try-catch block. Here's a basic example:

```
try {

// Code that may throw an exception

int result = 10 ~/ 0; // Division by zero will throw an exception

} catch (e) {

// Handle the exception

print('An error occurred: $e');

}
```

In this code, the division operation 10 ~/ 0 will throw a IntegerDivisionByZeroException exception. The catch block catches the exception and allows you to handle it gracefully.

You can specify different catch blocks to handle specific exception types:

```
try {

// Code that may throw an exception
```

```
} on IntegerDivisionByZeroException {
// Handle division by zero exception
print('Division by zero');
} on FormatException {
// Handle format exception
print('Invalid format');
} catch (e) {
// Handle other exceptions
print('An error occurred: $e');
}
```

The finally Block

You can use the finally block to specify code that will be executed regardless of whether an exception is thrown or not. It's often used for cleanup tasks, such as closing files or releasing resources.

```
try {
// Code that may throw an exception
} catch (e) {
// Handle the exception
print('An error occurred: $e');
} finally {
```

```
// Cleanup code
print('Cleanup');
}
```

Throwing Custom Exceptions

You can create your custom exceptions by extending the Exception class or any of its subclasses. This allows you to define custom exception types that are meaningful for your application.

```
class MyCustomException implements Exception {
final String message;
MyCustomException(this.message);
@override
String toString() => 'MyCustomException: $message';
}
```

Debugging Dart Code

Debugging is the process of identifying and fixing errors in your code. Dart provides several tools and techniques for debugging your applications.

Printing Debug Information

The simplest way to debug your code is by using print statements to output debug information to the console. You can print variable values, messages, and other relevant data to help you understand the flow of your program.

```
int age = 30;

print('Age: $age');
```

Using the Dart DevTools

Dart DevTools is a powerful debugging and profiling tool that provides a visual interface for debugging Flutter and Dart applications. You can use it to inspect the widget tree, view logs, and analyze the performance of your app.

To launch Dart DevTools, run the following command in your terminal while your Flutter app is running:

```
flutter pub global run devtools
```

Setting Breakpoints

In an integrated development environment (IDE) like Visual Studio Code or Android Studio, you can set breakpoints in your code. A breakpoint pauses the execution of your program at a specific line of code, allowing you to inspect variables and step through the code.

To set a breakpoint, click on the left margin of the code editor at the line where you want the program to pause.

Debugging with dartdev

You can also use the dartdev command-line tool to debug Dart applications. It provides features like stepping through code, inspecting variables, and evaluating expressions.

To start a Dart application in debug mode, use the following command:

dart—observe <your_app.dart>

This command starts your application and enables the Dart Observatory, which allows you to connect a debugger.

Conclusion

Exception handling and debugging are essential skills for Dart developers. By effectively handling exceptions and using debugging tools, you can write more reliable and bug-free Dart applications. Debugging helps you identify and fix issues in your code, ensuring that your applications run smoothly and provide a great user experience.

4.5. Advanced OOP Concepts in Dart

Dart is an object-oriented programming (OOP) language that supports various advanced OOP concepts to help you write clean and organized code. In this section, we'll delve into some of these advanced OOP concepts in Dart.

Inheritance and Polymorphism

Inheritance is a fundamental OOP concept that allows you to create a new class (the subclass or derived class) based on an existing class (the superclass or base class). The subclass inherits the properties and behaviors (methods and fields) of the superclass, allowing for code reuse and creating a hierarchy of classes.

class Animal {

String name;

Animal(this.name);

```
void speak() {
print('Animal speaks');
}
}
class Dog extends Animal {
Dog(String name) : super(name);
@override
void speak() {
print('$name barks');
}
}
void main() {
Animal myAnimal = Dog('Buddy');
myAnimal.speak(); // Calls Dog's speak method
}
```

In this example, Dog is a subclass of Animal. It inherits the name field and speak method from Animal. The @override annotation indicates that Dog is providing its own implementation of the speak method, which overrides the superclass method.

Polymorphism is the ability of objects of different classes to respond to the same method or property name in a way that is appropriate for their specific types. In the example above, myAnimal is of type

Animal, but it holds an instance of Dog. The speak method is called on myAnimal, and Dart's polymorphism ensures that the appropriate method for Dog is executed.

Abstract Classes and Interfaces

Abstract classes and **interfaces** are used to define common characteristics and behaviors that can be shared by multiple classes.

An **abstract class** is a class that cannot be instantiated directly and is typically used as a base class for other classes. It can contain abstract methods that must be implemented by its subclasses.

```
abstract class Shape {

double get area; // Abstract method

void displayArea() {

print('Area: $area');

}

}

class Circle extends Shape {

double radius;

Circle(this.radius);

@override

double get area => 3.14 * radius * radius;

}

void main() {
```

```
Circle circle = Circle(5);

circle.displayArea(); // Calls the abstract method implementation

}
```

In this example, Shape is an abstract class with an abstract method area. The Circle class extends Shape and provides an implementation of the area method.

An **interface** in Dart is defined using the implements keyword and specifies a contract that classes must adhere to by implementing its methods.

```
class Flyable {

void fly() {

print('Flying...');

}

}

class Bird implements Flyable {

@override

void fly() {

print('Bird is flying');

}

}

void main() {

Bird bird = Bird();
```

```
bird.fly(); // Calls the fly method from the Flyable interface
}
```

In this example, Bird implements the Flyable interface and provides its own implementation of the fly method.

Mixins

Mixins are a way to reuse a class's code in multiple class hierarchies. A mixin is a class that provides a set of methods and fields for use by other classes without becoming a parent class itself. To use a mixin, you include it in a class using the with keyword.

```
mixin LoggingMixin {
void log(String message) {
print('Log: $message');
}
}
class User with LoggingMixin {
String name;
User(this.name);
void display() {
log('User: $name');
}
}
void main() {
```

```
User user = User('Alice');

user.display();

}
```

In this example, LoggingMixin provides a log method, and the User class includes the mixin using with. This allows User objects to access the log method.

Conclusion

Dart's support for advanced OOP concepts like inheritance, polymorphism, abstract classes, interfaces, and mixins allows you to create well-structured and organized code. These concepts promote code reuse, maintainability, and extensibility, making Dart a powerful language for building complex applications with object-oriented design principles.

5. Crafting Beautiful UIs with Flutter

5.1. Theming and Styling Apps

Theming and styling play a crucial role in creating visually appealing and user-friendly Flutter applications. Flutter provides a powerful theming and styling system that allows you to customize the look and feel of your app to match your brand or design preferences. In this section, we'll explore how to use themes, apply custom styles, and create consistent and beautiful user interfaces in Flutter.

Using Themes in Flutter

Flutter's theming system is built around the concept of **themes**. A theme is a set of design choices that define the visual style of an app, such as colors, fonts, and shapes. Flutter uses a hierarchy of themes, with the top-level theme being the ThemeData provided by the app's MaterialApp widget. Themes can be customized at different levels, ensuring flexibility and consistency throughout your app.

Here's an example of how to define a custom theme for your app:

```
import 'package:flutter/material.dart';

void main() {

runApp(

MaterialApp(

theme: ThemeData(

primaryColor: Colors.blue,

accentColor: Colors.green,
```

```
fontFamily: 'Roboto',

// Add more theme properties as needed

),

home: MyHomePage(),

),

);

}
```

In this example, we set the primary color to blue, the accent color to green, and specify the font family as 'Roboto' for the entire app. These theme properties will be applied to various widgets, such as AppBar, Button, and Text, unless overridden explicitly.

Styling Widgets

To apply styles to individual widgets, you can use the style property or constructor arguments available in many Flutter widgets. For example, to style text, you can use the TextStyle class:

```
Text(

'Hello, World!',

style: TextStyle(

color: Colors.red,

fontSize: 20.0,

fontWeight: FontWeight.bold,

),
```

```
)
```

In this code, we set the text color to red, font size to 20, and font weight to bold.

Similarly, you can style other widgets like buttons, containers, and icons using their respective style properties or constructors.

Creating Custom Themes

Flutter allows you to create custom themes by extending the default ThemeData or by creating your custom ThemeData class. This enables you to define a unique visual style for your app.

```
import 'package:flutter/material.dart';

final customTheme = ThemeData(

primaryColor: Colors.purple,

accentColor: Colors.orange,

fontFamily: 'Montserrat',

// Add more custom theme properties here

);
```

You can then apply this custom theme to your app:

```
MaterialApp(

theme: customTheme,

home: MyHomePage(),

)
```

Dark Mode and Light Mode

Flutter makes it easy to support both dark mode and light mode in your app. You can define different themes for both modes and allow users to switch between them.

```
final lightTheme = ThemeData(

// Define light mode theme properties

);

final darkTheme = ThemeData(

// Define dark mode theme properties

);
```

To enable dark mode, you can use the MediaQuery to check the user's system settings:

```
final isDarkMode = MediaQuery.of(context).platformBrightness
== Brightness.dark;

return MaterialApp(

theme: isDarkMode ? darkTheme : lightTheme,

home: MyHomePage(),

);
```

Conclusion

Theming and styling are essential aspects of creating visually appealing and user-friendly Flutter applications. Flutter's theming system provides the flexibility to define custom themes, apply styles to widgets, and support both dark mode and light mode. By carefully designing your app's visual elements, you can create a consistent and beautiful user interface that enhances the overall user experience.

5.2. Animations and Transitions

Animations and transitions are powerful tools for enhancing the user experience in Flutter applications. They add interactivity, smoothness, and visual appeal to your app's user interface. In this section, we'll explore how to create animations and transitions in Flutter, from basic animations to complex transitions.

Basic Animations

Flutter provides several ways to create basic animations, including implicit animations, explicit animations, and physics-based animations.

Implicit animations are animations that are automatically handled by Flutter based on changes in widget properties. For example, the AnimatedContainer widget can animate its size, color, or alignment when its properties change:

```
AnimatedContainer(

duration: Duration(seconds: 1),

width: _isExpanded ? 200.0 : 100.0,

height: _isExpanded ? 100.0 : 50.0,

color: _isExpanded ? Colors.blue : Colors.red,

child: Center(child: Text('Animated Container')),

)
```

In this code, the container's properties (width, height, color) are animated when _isExpanded changes.

Explicit animations give you more control over the animation process. You can use widgets like AnimatedBuilder or TweenAnimationBuilder to create custom animations:

```
double _opacity = 1.0;

AnimatedBuilder(

animation: _controller,

builder: (context, child) {

return Opacity(

opacity: _opacity,

child: Text('Fading Text'),

);

},

)
```

In this example, _controller drives the animation, and the Opacity widget fades the text in and out.

Physics-based animations simulate physical motion using the PhysicsSimulation class. You can create realistic animations like bouncing, flinging, or springing:

```
SpringSimulation simulation = SpringSimulation(

SpringDescription(damping: 1.0, mass: 1.0, stiffness: 1.0),
```

```
_controller.value, // initial position

1.0, // target position

0.5, // initial velocity

);

controller.animateWith(simulation);
```

Transition Widgets

Flutter provides transition widgets that allow you to create smooth transitions between UI elements. Some common transition widgets include:

- SlideTransition: Slides a widget from one position to another.
- FadeTransition: Fades a widget in or out.
- RotationTransition: Rotates a widget during a transition.
- ScaleTransition: Scales a widget during a transition.

Here's an example of using SlideTransition to slide a widget:

```
SlideTransition(

position: _animation,

child: Text('Sliding Text'),

)
```

In this code, _animation controls the sliding motion of the text.

Complex Transitions

For more complex transitions, Flutter offers the Hero widget, which enables seamless transitions between widgets with matching hero tags. This is commonly used for transitioning between images in a gallery or between screens.

```
Hero(

tag: 'imageHero',

child: Image.asset('assets/image.png'),

)
```

To create a smooth transition, ensure that both the source and destination widgets have the same hero tag.

Conclusion

Animations and transitions are essential for creating engaging and visually appealing Flutter applications. Whether you're implementing basic animations, using transition widgets, or creating complex transitions with the Hero widget, Flutter provides a versatile set of tools to bring your app's user interface to life. Mastering these animation techniques can significantly enhance the overall user experience.

5.3. Using Custom Paint and Canvas

Custom Paint and Canvas are advanced Flutter features that allow you to create custom and intricate user interface elements and graphics. They provide the flexibility to draw shapes, patterns, and images directly onto the screen. In this section, we'll explore how to use Custom Paint and Canvas to create unique and visually stunning components for your Flutter applications.

Custom Paint Widget

The CustomPaint widget is the foundation for creating custom graphics in Flutter. It allows you to specify a CustomPainter that defines how to paint on the screen. Here's a simple example:

```
CustomPaint(

painter: MyPainter(),

child: Container(

width: 200,

height: 200,

),

)
```

In this code, MyPainter is a custom painter class that you'll need to define. It determines what is painted within the CustomPaint widget.

CustomPainter Class

The CustomPainter class is where you define the logic for drawing on the canvas. To create a custom painter, you need to extend the CustomPainter class and implement the paint and shouldRepaint methods.

```
class MyPainter extends CustomPainter {

@override
```

```
void paint(Canvas canvas, Size size) {
final paint = Paint()
..color = Colors.blue
..strokeCap = StrokeCap.round
..strokeWidth = 5.0;
final center = size.center(Offset.zero);
canvas.drawLine(center, Offset(center.dx, center.dy - 50), paint);
}
@override
bool shouldRepaint(covariant CustomPainter oldDelegate) {
return false;
}
}
```

In this example, the paint method is used to draw a blue line on the canvas. The shouldRepaint method should return true if the painter should be repainted when the widget changes, or false if it should not.

Drawing Shapes and Paths

With Custom Paint and Canvas, you can draw various shapes and paths, including lines, circles, rectangles, and more. For example, to draw a circle:

```
canvas.drawCircle(center, 50, paint);
```

To draw a rectangle:

```
final rect = Rect.fromCenter(center: center, width: 100, height: 80);

canvas.drawRect(rect, paint);
```

Custom Clipping

Custom Paint and Canvas also allow for custom clipping, enabling you to create non-rectangular shapes. You can use the clipPath method to define a custom clipping path and then draw within that path.

Performance Considerations

While Custom Paint and Canvas offer great flexibility, they should be used judiciously as they can have performance implications, especially for complex graphics. Flutter provides the RepaintBoundary widget to isolate custom painted elements, which can help optimize performance by reducing unnecessary repaints.

Conclusion

Custom Paint and Canvas in Flutter provide the means to create custom graphics, visual effects, and unique user interface components. With these tools, you can unleash your creativity to design interactive and visually striking elements that enhance the overall look and feel of your Flutter applications. However, it's essential to be mindful of performance considerations when working with custom graphics.

5.4. Responsive Design: Adapting UI for Different Devices

Creating a responsive user interface is crucial for ensuring that your Flutter app looks and functions well on a variety of devices, including smartphones, tablets, and desktops. In this section, we'll explore strategies and techniques for designing responsive Flutter applications that adapt to different screen sizes and orientations.

MediaQuery and LayoutBuilder

Flutter provides two essential tools for designing responsive layouts: MediaQuery and LayoutBuilder.

MediaQuery allows you to retrieve information about the device's screen size, orientation, and more. You can use it to conditionally adapt your UI elements based on the screen's characteristics.

```
final width = MediaQuery.of(context).size.width;

if (width < 600) {

// Adjust UI for small screens

} else {

// Adjust UI for larger screens

}
```

LayoutBuilder is a widget that provides constraints to its child based on the parent widget's size. This is helpful for creating flexible layouts that adapt to available space.

```
LayoutBuilder(

builder: (context, constraints) {
```

```
if (constraints.maxWidth < 600) {

// Adjust UI for narrow layouts

} else {

// Adjust UI for wider layouts

}

},

)
```

Responsive Layouts with Rows and Columns

Flutter's Row and Column widgets are versatile for creating responsive layouts. You can use the Expanded widget within rows and columns to distribute available space proportionally.

```
Row(

children: [

Expanded(

flex: 2,

child: Container(

color: Colors.red,

height: 100,

),

),

Expanded(
```

```
flex: 3,
child: Container(
color: Colors.blue,
height: 100,
),
),
],
)
```

In this example, the first container takes up 2/5 of the available horizontal space, while the second container takes up 3/5.

Adaptive Widgets

Flutter offers adaptive widgets that automatically adapt to the device's platform and screen size. For example, you can use CupertinoButton and ElevatedButton to create platform-specific buttons:

```
Platform.isIOS
? CupertinoButton(
child: Text('iOS Button'),
onPressed: () {},
)
: ElevatedButton(
onPressed: () {},
```

```
child: Text('Android Button'),
)
```

Similarly, the Scaffold widget adapts its appearance based on the platform, ensuring a native look and feel.

Orientation Changes

Handling orientation changes is essential for responsive design. You can use the OrientationBuilder widget to respond to changes in device orientation:

```
OrientationBuilder(
builder: (context, orientation) {
if (orientation == Orientation.portrait) {
// Adjust UI for portrait orientation
} else {
// Adjust UI for landscape orientation
}
},
)
```

Conclusion

Designing responsive Flutter applications involves using MediaQuery, LayoutBuilder, flexible layouts, adaptive widgets, and handling orientation changes. By implementing these techniques, you can create user interfaces that adapt seamlessly to various screen sizes and orientations, providing an optimal user experience on different devices.

5.5. Accessibility and Internationalization

Accessibility and internationalization are essential aspects of creating inclusive and user-friendly Flutter applications. In this section, we'll explore how to make your Flutter app more accessible to users with disabilities and how to support multiple languages and regions for a global audience.

Accessibility in Flutter

Accessibility ensures that your app can be used by individuals with disabilities, such as vision impairments. Flutter provides built-in support for accessibility through the Semantics widget and the AccessibilityNode class.

Semantics Widget: The Semantics widget is used to add semantic information to your app's UI elements. This information helps screen readers provide spoken feedback to users with disabilities. For example:

```
Semantics(
label: 'Submit Button',
child: ElevatedButton(
onPressed: () {},
child: Text('Submit'),
),
)
```

In this code, the label property provides a description of the button, making it accessible to screen readers.

AccessibilityNode: You can use the AccessibilityNode class to provide custom accessibility information. For example, you can set accessibility labels, hints, and roles for widgets:

```
final node = AccessibilityNodeInfo();

node.label = 'Close Button';

node.hint = 'Tap to close';

node.role = AccessibilityRole.button;

Accessibility.attachAccessibilityNodeInfo(

buttonKey.currentContext!,

node,

);
```

By using these accessibility features, you can ensure that users with disabilities can navigate and interact with your app effectively.

Internationalization in Flutter

Internationalization, often referred to as i18n, is the process of adapting your app to support multiple languages and regions. Flutter makes internationalization straightforward through the intl package and localization widgets.

intl Package: The intl package provides tools for working with dates, times, currencies, and translations. You can format dates and numbers based on the user's locale:

```
final formattedDate = DateFormat.yMd().format(DateTime.now());

final formattedCurrency = NumberFormat.currency(locale: 'en_US').format(1000);
```

Localization Widgets: Flutter offers widgets like Localizations and MaterialApp that support app-wide localization. You can use the Localizations widget to access translated strings:

```
Text(

AppLocalizations.of(context).translate('hello_message'),

)
```

Supporting Multiple Languages

To support multiple languages, you'll need to provide translation files for each language. Flutter uses the arb (Application Resource Bundle) format for managing translations. You can use tools like the intl_translation package to extract and manage translation messages.

RTL (Right-to-Left) Support

For languages that are written from right to left (e.g., Arabic, Hebrew), Flutter provides support for mirroring the user interface. You can enable RTL support using the Directionality widget:

```
Directionality(

textDirection: TextDirection.rtl,

child: Text('مرحباً بك'),

)
```

Conclusion

Accessibility and internationalization are crucial for making your Flutter app inclusive and accessible to a global audience. By implementing accessibility features like the Semantics widget and providing internationalization support through the intl package and localization widgets, you can ensure that your app is usable and culturally relevant to users around the world, including those with disabilities.

Chapter 6: State Management in Flutter

6.1. Understanding the Need for State Management

State management is a critical aspect of building Flutter applications, especially as your app grows in complexity. In this section, we'll delve into the importance of state management and why it's necessary for developing efficient and responsive Flutter apps.

What Is State?

In Flutter, "state" refers to the data that an app needs to keep track of to function correctly. This data can include user inputs, the current screen, network requests, and more. Flutter's UI is built using a declarative approach, meaning the UI is a direct function of the app's current state. When the state changes, the UI updates to reflect those changes.

The Need for State Management

As your Flutter app becomes more feature-rich, managing state becomes increasingly challenging. Without proper state management, you may encounter issues like:

1. **UI Inconsistencies**: Without a clear and organized way to manage state, you might end up with UI elements that don't reflect the correct data or have conflicting states.
2. **Code Complexity**: State management helps you organize and centralize your app's data. Without it, your code can become complex and difficult to maintain, leading to bugs and reduced productivity.
3. **Performance Problems**: Inefficient state management can

result in unnecessary UI updates, causing performance bottlenecks and impacting the user experience.

4. **Scalability Challenges**: As your app scales, managing state becomes even more critical. A lack of proper state management can hinder your ability to add new features and maintain a stable app.

Types of State in Flutter

In Flutter, there are primarily two types of state:

1. **Ephemeral State**: Also known as local state, this type of state is short-lived and specific to a single widget or screen. It doesn't need to be shared across the app.
2. **App State**: App-wide or global state is data that needs to be accessible from multiple parts of your app. It typically includes data that needs to persist across various screens and widgets.

Approaches to State Management

Flutter offers several approaches to state management, each with its own strengths and use cases. Some popular state management solutions include:

- **Provider**: Provider is a straightforward and efficient way to manage state using a lightweight, built-in package. It's suitable for both small and large applications.

- **Riverpod**: Riverpod is built on top of Provider and offers more advanced features like dependency injection and a powerful way to manage app state.

- **Bloc Pattern**: The Bloc pattern is a design pattern for managing state using streams and events. It's a robust solution for complex apps with intricate state management needs.

- **Redux**: Redux is a predictable state container for Dart that helps manage app state in a consistent and organized manner. It's ideal for apps with a large amount of shared state.

- **GetX**: GetX is a popular package that provides simple and high-performance state management, along with routing and dependency injection.

Conclusion

Understanding the importance of state management is fundamental to becoming proficient in Flutter development. It's a critical skill that allows you to build responsive and maintainable apps. As you explore the different state management solutions available in Flutter, you'll be better equipped to choose the one that fits your project's needs. In the following sections of this chapter, we'll dive deeper into specific state management techniques and how to implement them in your Flutter app.

6.2. Exploring Provider and Riverpod

In the world of Flutter state management, Provider and Riverpod are two powerful and popular packages that simplify the process of managing state within your app. In this section, we'll explore both of these packages, their differences, and how to use them effectively.

Provider

Provider is an officially recommended package for state management in Flutter. It's known for its simplicity and ease of use. Provider is built on top of InheritedWidget and uses the concept of "provider" to make your app's state available to different parts of the widget tree.

Here's a basic example of how to use Provider:

```
// Import the necessary packages.

import 'package:flutter/material.dart';

import 'package:provider/provider.dart';

// Create a class to represent your app's state.

class CounterModel extends ChangeNotifier {

int count = 0;

void increment() {

count++;

notifyListeners(); // Notifies the listeners that the state has changed.

}

}

void main() {

runApp(

ChangeNotifierProvider(

create: (context) => CounterModel(), // Provide an instance of your state class.
```

```
child: MyApp(),
),
);
}
class MyApp extends StatelessWidget {
@override
Widget build(BuildContext context) {
return MaterialApp(
home: Scaffold(
appBar: AppBar(
title: Text('Provider Example'),
),
body: Center(
child: Column(
mainAxisAlignment: MainAxisAlignment.center,
children: <Widget>[
Text(
'Counter Value:',
),
Consumer<CounterModel>(
```

```
builder: (context, counter, child) => Text(
'${counter.count}', // Access the state using Provider.
style: TextStyle(fontSize: 24),
),
),
RaisedButton(
onPressed: () {
Provider.of<CounterModel>(context, listen: false).increment();
},
child: Text('Increment'),
),
],
),
),
),
);
}
}
```

In this example, we create a simple counter app using Provider. The CounterModel class represents our app's state, and we use the ChangeNotifier mixin to notify listeners when the state changes. We then wrap our app with ChangeNotifierProvider, which provides an instance of CounterModel to the widget tree.

Riverpod

Riverpod is built on top of Provider and extends its capabilities. It offers more advanced features, including improved dependency injection and a more granular approach to state management. Riverpod is designed to be scalable and testable.

Here's a brief example of how Riverpod works:

```
import 'package:flutter/material.dart';

import 'package:flutter_riverpod/flutter_riverpod.dart';

final counterProvider = StateNotifierProvider<CounterNotifier, int>((ref) {

return CounterNotifier();

});

class CounterNotifier extends StateNotifier<int> {

CounterNotifier() : super(0);

void increment() {

state++;

}

}

void main() {

runApp(
```

```
ProviderScope(
child: MyApp(),
),
);
}
class MyApp extends StatelessWidget {
@override
Widget build(BuildContext context) {
return MaterialApp(
home: Scaffold(
appBar: AppBar(
title: Text('Riverpod Example'),
),
body: Center(
child: Column(
mainAxisAlignment: MainAxisAlignment.center,
children: <Widget>[
Text(
'Counter Value:',
),
```

```
Consumer(
builder: (context, watch, child) {
final counter = watch(counterProvider);
return Text(
'$counter',
style: TextStyle(fontSize: 24),
);
},
),
RaisedButton(
onPressed: () {
context.read(counterProvider.notifier).increment();
},
child: Text('Increment'),
),
],
),
),
),
);
```

```
}
}
```

In this Riverpod example, we define a counterProvider using StateNotifierProvider, which encapsulates our app's state and logic. The ProviderScope widget ensures that Riverpod providers are available throughout the widget tree. We use the Consumer widget to access and rebuild the UI when the state changes.

Choosing Between Provider and Riverpod

The choice between Provider and Riverpod depends on your project's requirements and complexity. Provider is straightforward and suitable for most cases, while Riverpod offers more advanced features and is a better fit for larger and more complex applications.

When deciding, consider factors like the size of your app, the need for advanced dependency injection, and your familiarity with the packages. Both Provider and Riverpod are excellent choices for state management in Flutter, and you can't go wrong with either one.

6.3. Bloc Pattern: Theory and Implementation

The Bloc (Business Logic Component) pattern is a design pattern that plays a significant role in state management in Flutter applications. It separates the business logic from the UI layer, making it easier to manage complex state and interactions. In this section, we'll delve into the theory behind the Bloc pattern and demonstrate its implementation in Flutter.

Understanding the Bloc Pattern

The Bloc pattern follows a simple and clear architecture:

- **Events**: These are the inputs to the Bloc. Events represent actions or triggers that can change the state.
- **Bloc**: The Bloc is responsible for processing events, applying business logic, and emitting new states. It doesn't depend on the UI and is independent of it.
- **States**: States represent the different states that your application can be in. Each event processed by the Bloc can result in a state change.
- **UI Layer**: The UI layer listens to state changes and updates the user interface accordingly. It doesn't contain business logic.

The key idea is that the UI layer doesn't have direct access to the business logic or state. Instead, it communicates with the Bloc through events and reacts to state changes emitted by the Bloc.

Implementation of Bloc in Flutter

Let's implement a simple counter app using the Bloc pattern in Flutter. We'll use the bloc package for this demonstration.

First, add the bloc package to your pubspec.yaml file:

dependencies:

flutter:

sdk: flutter

bloc: ^7.0.0 # *Use the latest version of the bloc package.*

Now, let's create the Bloc, events, and states:

```
import 'package:bloc/bloc.dart';

import 'package:equatable/equatable.dart';

// Define the events

abstract class CounterEvent extends Equatable {

const CounterEvent();

@override

List<Object?> get props => [];

}

class IncrementEvent extends CounterEvent {}

class DecrementEvent extends CounterEvent {}

// Define the states

abstract class CounterState extends Equatable {

const CounterState();

@override

List<Object?> get props => [];

}

class InitialState extends CounterState {

final int count;
```

```
InitialState(this.count);

@override

List<Object?> get props => [count];

}

// Create the Bloc

class CounterBloc extends Bloc<CounterEvent, CounterState> {

CounterBloc() : super(InitialState(0));

@override

Stream<CounterState> mapEventToState(CounterEvent event) async* {

if (event is IncrementEvent) {

yield InitialState(state.count + 1);

} else if (event is DecrementEvent) {

yield InitialState(state.count - 1);

}

}

}
```

In this code, we define two events (IncrementEvent and DecrementEvent) and two states (InitialState) for our counter app. The CounterBloc class extends Bloc and defines how events map to states. When an event is dispatched, it triggers the corresponding state change.

Now, let's create the UI:

```
import 'package:flutter/material.dart';

import 'package:flutter_bloc/flutter_bloc.dart';

void main() {

runApp(MyApp());

}

class MyApp extends StatelessWidget {

@override

Widget build(BuildContext context) {

return MaterialApp(

home: BlocProvider(

create: (context) => CounterBloc(),

child: CounterPage(),

),

);

}

}

class CounterPage extends StatelessWidget {

@override

Widget build(BuildContext context) {
```

```
final counterBloc = BlocProvider.of<CounterBloc>(context);
return Scaffold(
appBar: AppBar(
title: Text('Bloc Pattern Example'),
),
body: Center(
child: Column(
mainAxisAlignment: MainAxisAlignment.center,
children: <Widget>[
Text(
'Counter Value:',
),
BlocBuilder<CounterBloc, CounterState>(
builder: (context, state) {
if (state is InitialState) {
return Text(
'${state.count}',
style: TextStyle(fontSize: 24),
);
}
```

```
return Container(); // Placeholder for other states.
},
),
Row(
mainAxisAlignment: MainAxisAlignment.center,
children: <Widget>[
RaisedButton(
onPressed: () {
counterBloc.add(IncrementEvent());
},
child: Text('Increment'),
),
SizedBox(width: 16),
RaisedButton(
onPressed: () {
counterBloc.add(DecrementEvent());
},
child: Text('Decrement'),
),
],
```

```
),
],
),
),
);
}
}
```

In this code, we create the UI using BlocBuilder, which listens to state changes emitted by the CounterBloc. When the user taps the "Increment" or "Decrement" button, the corresponding event is dispatched to the Bloc, triggering state changes.

The Bloc pattern's clear separation of concerns and the unidirectional data flow it offers make it a powerful choice for state management in Flutter applications, especially for larger and more complex projects. It promotes maintainability, testability, and scalability while keeping your UI layer clean and responsive.

6.4. Redux in Flutter

Redux is another popular state management pattern that originated from the web development world and has found its way into Flutter applications. It follows the principles of a single immutable state tree and actions to modify the state. In this section, we'll explore how to implement Redux in Flutter.

Understanding Redux Principles

Redux follows a set of core principles:

1. **Single Immutable State**: In Redux, your entire application state is stored in a single, immutable object. This makes it easy to track changes and maintain a consistent application state.
2. **Actions**: Actions are plain objects that describe what happened. They are the only way to modify the state in Redux. Actions are dispatched to trigger state changes.
3. **Reducers**: Reducers are pure functions that specify how the state changes in response to an action. They take the current state and an action and return the new state.
4. **Store**: The store holds the application state, allows access to it, and provides a way to dispatch actions. It is the central hub of Redux.

Implementing Redux in Flutter

To implement Redux in Flutter, you can use packages like redux and flutter_redux. Here's a basic example of how to set up Redux:

1. Add the redux and flutter_redux packages to your pubspec.yaml file:

```
dependencies:

flutter:

sdk: flutter

redux: ^4.0.0

flutter_redux: ^0.9.5
```

1. Define your actions and reducers:

```
// actions.dart
```

```
class IncrementAction {}

class DecrementAction {}

// reducers.dart

int counterReducer(int state, dynamic action) {

if (action is IncrementAction) {

return state + 1;

} else if (action is DecrementAction) {

return state - 1;

}

return state;

}
```

1. Create the Redux store and wrap your app with the StoreProvider:

```
// main.dart

import 'package:flutter/material.dart';

import 'package:flutter_redux/flutter_redux.dart';

import 'package:redux/redux.dart';

import 'actions.dart';

import 'reducers.dart';

void main() {
```

```
final store = Store<int>(
counterReducer,
initialState: 0,
);
runApp(MyApp(store: store));
}
class MyApp extends StatelessWidget {
final Store<int> store;
MyApp({required this.store});
@override
Widget build(BuildContext context) {
return StoreProvider<int>(
store: store,
child: MaterialApp(
home: CounterPage(),
),
);
}
}
```

1. Build your UI and connect it to the Redux store using

StoreConnector:

```
// counter_page.dart
import 'package:flutter/material.dart';
import 'package:flutter_redux/flutter_redux.dart';
import 'package:redux/redux.dart';
import 'actions.dart';
class CounterPage extends StatelessWidget {
@override
Widget build(BuildContext context) {
return Scaffold(
appBar: AppBar(
title: Text('Redux Example'),
),
body: Center(
child: Column(
mainAxisAlignment: MainAxisAlignment.center,
children: <Widget>[
Text(
'Counter Value:',
),
```

```
StoreConnector<int, int>(
converter: (Store<int> store) => store.state,
builder: (BuildContext context, int count) {
return Text(
'$count',
style: TextStyle(fontSize: 24),
);
},
),
Row(
mainAxisAlignment: MainAxisAlignment.center,
children: <Widget>[
StoreConnector<int, VoidCallback>(
converter: (Store<int> store) {
return () => store.dispatch(IncrementAction());
},
builder: (BuildContext context, VoidCallback callback) {
return RaisedButton(
onPressed: callback,
child: Text('Increment'),
```

```
);
},
),
SizedBox(width: 16),
StoreConnector<int, VoidCallback>(
converter: (Store<int> store) {
return () => store.dispatch(DecrementAction());
},
builder: (BuildContext context, VoidCallback callback) {
return RaisedButton(
onPressed: callback,
child: Text('Decrement'),
);
},
),
],
),
],
),
),
```

```
);
}
}
```

In this Redux implementation, we define actions, reducers, create a Redux store, and connect our UI using StoreProvider and StoreConnector. The store holds the application state, and actions dispatched by buttons trigger state changes through reducers.

Redux is particularly useful for managing complex application states and helps maintain a predictable and traceable flow of data. While it may introduce more code compared to other state management approaches, it pays off in terms of scalability and maintainability for larger applications.

6.5. Advanced State Management Techniques

While Flutter offers various state management options, some scenarios may require more advanced techniques to handle complex application states efficiently. In this section, we'll explore some advanced state management techniques in Flutter.

1. Using ChangeNotifierProxyProvider for Combined Providers

In scenarios where you need to combine data from multiple providers and expose a single, aggregated provider, you can use ChangeNotifierProxyProvider. This provider allows you to access and modify multiple providers and create a new provider based on their values.

Here's an example:

```
ChangeNotifierProxyProvider2<ProviderA, ProviderB, CombinedProvider>(

create: (context) => CombinedProvider(),

update: (context, providerA, providerB, combinedProvider) {

combinedProvider.updateData(providerA.data, providerB.data);

return combinedProvider;

},

child: MyApp(),

);
```

2. Using flutter_bloc for Complex Business Logic

If your app involves complex business logic, consider using the flutter_bloc package. It implements the BLoC (Business Logic Component) pattern, separating the UI from the business logic. It's particularly useful for applications with intricate state transitions.

```
class CounterCubit extends Cubit<int> {

CounterCubit() : super(0);

void increment() => emit(state + 1);

void decrement() => emit(state - 1);

}

// In your widget:

BlocProvider(

create: (context) => CounterCubit(),
```

```
child: CounterPage(),

);
```

3. Leveraging StreamBuilder for Real-Time Updates

When working with real-time data streams, you can use the StreamBuilder widget to efficiently update your UI as data changes. This is especially helpful for features like chat applications, live scoreboards, or any scenario involving continuous data updates.

```
StreamBuilder<List<Message>>(

stream: messageStream,

builder: (context, snapshot) {

if (!snapshot.hasData) {

return CircularProgressIndicator();

}

final messages = snapshot.data;

return ListView.builder(

itemCount: messages.length,

itemBuilder: (context, index) {

return MessageItem(messages[index]);

},

);

},
```

```
);
```

4. Implementing Middleware for Side Effects

Middleware can be used to perform side effects like logging, analytics, or making network requests in response to actions. The redux package provides a middleware mechanism for this purpose.

```
final store = Store<int>(

counterReducer,

initialState: 0,

middleware: [loggerMiddleware],

);
```

5. Managing Navigation State

For applications with complex navigation requirements, managing the navigation state can become challenging. You can use packages like provider or flutter_bloc to handle navigation state and easily navigate between screens while maintaining a clear separation of concerns.

```
Navigator(

pages: [

MaterialPage(child: HomeScreen()),

if (showDetails) MaterialPage(child: DetailsScreen()),

],

onPopPage: (route, result) {
```

```
// Handle pop operations here

return route.didPop(result);

},

);
```

These advanced state management techniques can help you handle more complex scenarios and maintain a scalable and maintainable codebase as your Flutter application grows in complexity. Remember to choose the technique that best fits your app's specific requirements and complexity level.

7.1. Making HTTP Requests and Parsing JSON

In modern mobile app development, making HTTP requests and handling JSON data is a common task. Flutter provides excellent tools and libraries for performing these operations efficiently. In this section, we'll explore how to make HTTP requests and parse JSON data in your Flutter applications.

1. Using the http Package

Flutter offers the http package, a widely-used library for making HTTP requests. To use it, add the package to your pubspec.yaml:

```
dependencies:

http: ^0.13.3
```

After adding the package, you can perform HTTP GET requests like this:

```
import 'package:http/http.dart' as http;
```

```
Future<void> fetchData() async {

final response = await http.get(Uri.parse('https://api.example.com/
data'));

if (response.statusCode == 200) {

print('Response data: ${response.body}');

} else {

throw Exception('Failed to load data');

}

}
```

2. Parsing JSON Data

To parse JSON data, you can use Flutter's built-in support for converting JSON strings to Dart objects. Typically, you'll create Dart classes to represent the JSON structure.

```
import 'dart:convert';

class User {

final int id;

final String name;

User({required this.id, required this.name});

factory User.fromJson(Map<String, dynamic> json) {

return User(

id: json['id'],
```

```
name: json['name'],
);
}
}
void parseJson(String jsonString) {
final Map<String, dynamic> data = json.decode(jsonString);
final user = User.fromJson(data);
print('User ID: ${user.id}, Name: ${user.name}');
}
```

3. Handling Asynchronous Operations

HTTP requests and JSON parsing are asynchronous operations. You should use async and await to ensure your app remains responsive while performing these tasks.

```
Future<void> fetchData() async {
try {
final response = await http.get(Uri.parse('https://api.example.com/data'));
if (response.statusCode == 200) {
final data = json.decode(response.body);
print('Response data: $data');
} else {
```

```
throw Exception('Failed to load data');

}

} catch (e) {

print('Error: $e');

}

}
```

4. Handling Network Connectivity

It's important to handle network connectivity and errors gracefully. The connectivity package can help you monitor and react to changes in network status.

```
import 'package:connectivity/connectivity.dart';

final connectivity = Connectivity();

StreamSubscription<ConnectivityResult> subscription;

void initConnectivity() {

subscription = connectivity.onConnectivityChanged.listen((result)
{

if (result == ConnectivityResult.none) {

// No network connection

} else if (result == ConnectivityResult.wifi) {

// Connected to Wi-Fi

} else if (result == ConnectivityResult.mobile) {
```

```
// Connected to mobile data
}
});
}
void disposeConnectivity() {
subscription.cancel();
}
```

5. Making POST Requests and Sending Data

In addition to GET requests, you can also make POST requests to send data to a server. Use the http.post method and pass data in the request body.

```
final response = await http.post(
Uri.parse('https://api.example.com/postData'),
body: jsonEncode({'key': 'value'}),
headers: {'Content-Type': 'application/json'},
);
```

Making HTTP requests and parsing JSON data is fundamental for building data-driven Flutter applications. The http package and JSON serialization provide the tools you need to communicate with APIs, retrieve data, and display it in your app.

7.2. Working with Local Storage

Storing data locally is a common requirement in Flutter applications. Whether you need to save user preferences, cache data, or store information for offline use, Flutter provides various options for working with local storage. In this section, we'll explore different techniques and packages for handling local storage in Flutter.

1. Using Shared Preferences

The shared_preferences package is a simple and straightforward way to store key-value pairs locally, such as user preferences or settings. To use it, add the package to your pubspec.yaml:

```
dependencies:

shared_preferences: ^2.0.12
```

Here's how you can use shared_preferences to store and retrieve data:

```
import 'package:shared_preferences/shared_preferences.dart';

Future<void> savePreferences() async {

final prefs = await SharedPreferences.getInstance();

prefs.setString('username', 'example_user');

}

Future<String?> getSavedUsername() async {

final prefs = await SharedPreferences.getInstance();

return prefs.getString('username');

}
```

2. Using Local Database with sqflite

For more structured and complex data storage needs, you can use a local database. The sqflite package provides a SQLite-based local database for Flutter apps. To use it, add the package to your pubspec.yaml:

```
dependencies:

sqflite: ^2.0.0

path: ^2.0.1
```

Here's an example of how to create and interact with a SQLite database:

```
import 'package:sqflite/sqflite.dart';

import 'package:path/path.dart';

Future<Database> openDatabase() async {

final databasePath = await getDatabasesPath();

final path = join(databasePath, 'my_database.db');

return openDatabase(path, version: 1, onCreate: (db, version) {

// Create tables and define schema here

db.execute('CREATE TABLE users (id INTEGER PRIMARY KEY, name TEXT)');

});

}

Future<void> insertUser(User user) async {
```

```
final db = await openDatabase();
await db.insert('users', user.toMap());
}
Future<List<User>> getUsers() async {
final db = await openDatabase();
final List<Map<String, dynamic>> maps = await db.query('users');
return List.generate(maps.length, (i) {
return User(
id: maps[i]['id'],
name: maps[i]['name'],
);
});
}
```

3. Using Hive for NoSQL Data Storage

If you prefer a NoSQL approach to local storage, you can use the hive package. Hive is a lightweight and fast key-value store for Flutter. To use it, add the package to your pubspec.yaml:

```
dependencies:
hive: ^2.0.4
hive_flutter: ^1.0.0
```

Here's an example of how to work with Hive:

```
import 'package:hive/hive.dart';

void initializeHive() async {

await Hive.initFlutter();

await Hive.openBox('myBox');

}

void saveData() {

final box = Hive.box('myBox');

box.put('key', 'value');

}

String? retrieveData() {

final box = Hive.box('myBox');

return box.get('key');

}
```

4. File-Based Storage

Sometimes, you may need to store and retrieve files, such as images or documents, locally. Flutter's path_provider package can help you access directories for file storage.

```
dependencies:

path_provider: ^2.0.3
```

Here's an example of how to use path_provider:

```
import 'package:path_provider/path_provider.dart';
```

```
import 'dart:io';

Future<String> getLocalFilePath() async {

final directory = await getApplicationDocumentsDirectory();

return directory.path;

}

Future<File> createFile(String filename) async {

final path = await getLocalFilePath();

return File('$path/$filename');

}
```

Working with local storage is crucial for managing user data and optimizing your Flutter app's performance. Depending on your specific requirements, you can choose the appropriate storage solution, whether it's simple key-value pairs, SQLite databases, NoSQL storage, or file-based storage.

7.3. Integrating Databases with Flutter

In many Flutter applications, you may need to work with databases to store, retrieve, and manage structured data efficiently. Databases are crucial for applications that involve user accounts, product catalogs, messages, or any other form of persistent data. Flutter provides several options for integrating databases into your app, and in this section, we'll explore some common approaches.

1. Using sqflite for SQLite Databases

sqflite is a popular and well-maintained package for working with SQLite databases in Flutter. SQLite is a lightweight, file-based, embedded database engine that is ideal for mobile applications. To use sqflite, add it to your pubspec.yaml file:

```
dependencies:

sqflite: ^2.0.0

path: ^2.0.1
```

Here's a basic example of how to create, insert, retrieve, and update data in an SQLite database using sqflite:

```
import 'package:sqflite/sqflite.dart';

import 'package:path/path.dart';

Future<Database> openDatabase() async {

final databasePath = await getDatabasesPath();

final path = join(databasePath, 'my_database.db');

return openDatabase(path, version: 1, onCreate: (db, version) {

// Create tables and define schema here

db.execute('CREATE TABLE users (id INTEGER PRIMARY KEY, name TEXT)');

});

}

Future<void> insertUser(User user) async {
```

```
final db = await openDatabase();
await db.insert('users', user.toMap());
}
Future<List<User>> getUsers() async {
final db = await openDatabase();
final List<Map<String, dynamic>> maps = await db.query('users');
return List.generate(maps.length, (i) {
return User(
id: maps[i]['id'],
name: maps[i]['name'],
);
});
}
```

2. Using Object-Relational Mapping (ORM)

Object-Relational Mapping (ORM) libraries like moor and sqfentity provide a higher-level, more intuitive way to work with databases in Flutter. These libraries allow you to define your database schema using Dart classes and generate database-related code automatically.

Example using moor:

```
dependencies:
```

```
moor: ^4.8.0

moor_flutter: ^4.8.0

import 'package:moor/moor.dart';

import 'package:moor_flutter/moor_flutter.dart';

@DataClassName('User')

class Users extends Table {

IntColumn get id => integer().autoIncrement()();

TextColumn get name => text()();

}

@UseMoor(tables: [Users])

class AppDatabase extends _$AppDatabase {

AppDatabase(QueryExecutor e) : super(e);

@override

int get schemaVersion => 1;

}

Future<void> insertUser(AppDatabase database, User user) {

return database.into(database.users).insert(user);

}

Future<List<User>> getUsers(AppDatabase database) {

return database.select(database.users).get();
```

}

3. Using Hive for NoSQL Data Storage

If you prefer a NoSQL approach to data storage, you can use the hive package. Hive is a fast and lightweight key-value store for Flutter that allows you to store structured data in a simple, efficient way. To use hive, add it to your pubspec.yaml file:

```
dependencies:

hive: ^2.0.4

hive_flutter: ^1.0.0
```

Here's an example of using Hive to define and work with a custom data model:

```
import 'package:hive/hive.dart';

part 'person.g.dart';

@HiveType(typeId: 0)

class Person extends HiveObject {

@HiveField(0)

late String name;

@HiveField(1)

late int age;

}
```

Working with databases in Flutter gives you the ability to manage and manipulate data efficiently. Depending on your project's requirements and complexity, you can choose between SQLite databases with sqflite, ORM libraries like moor or sqfentity, or the simplicity of Hive for NoSQL data storage. Each approach has its advantages and may be more suitable for different use cases.

7.4. Securing Data and Privacy Considerations

Ensuring the security and privacy of user data is paramount when developing Flutter applications, especially when dealing with sensitive information. In this section, we will explore various strategies and best practices to secure data and address privacy concerns in your Flutter apps.

1. Data Encryption

Encrypting data at rest and during transit is a fundamental security measure. Flutter provides packages and libraries for implementing data encryption.

Example using the encrypt package:

```
dependencies:

encrypt: ^5.0.1

import 'package:encrypt/encrypt.dart';

void encryptAndDecryptData() {

final key = Key.fromUtf8('my_secret_key_123'); // Replace with a strong, unique key

final iv = IV.fromLength(16); // Initialization Vector
```

```
final encrypter = Encrypter(AES(key, iv));

final plainText = 'Sensitive data to be encrypted';

final encrypted = encrypter.encrypt(plainText, iv: iv);

final decrypted = encrypter.decrypt(encrypted, iv: iv);

print('Original: $plainText');

print('Encrypted: ${encrypted.base64}');

print('Decrypted: $decrypted');

}
```

2. User Authentication

Implement secure user authentication to verify the identity of users accessing your app. Utilize authentication providers like Firebase Authentication, OAuth, or custom solutions with proper password hashing and salting techniques.

Example using Firebase Authentication:

```
dependencies:

firebase_auth: ^4.3.0

import 'package:firebase_auth/firebase_auth.dart';

Future<void> signInWithEmailAndPassword() async {

try {

final userCredential = await FirebaseAuth.instance.signInWithEmailAndPassword(
```

```
email: 'user@email.com',
password: 'password123',
);
final user = userCredential.user;
print('Signed in as ${user?.uid}');
} catch (e) {
print('Authentication failed: $e');
}
}
```

3. Data Validation and Sanitization

Always validate and sanitize user inputs to prevent injection attacks, such as SQL injection and cross-site scripting (XSS). Use packages like validators or implement custom validation logic.

Example using the validators package:

```
dependencies:
validators: ^3.0.0
import 'package:validators/validators.dart';
bool isEmailValid(String email) {
return isEmail(email);
}
```

4. Permissions and Access Control

Request only the necessary permissions from users, following the principle of least privilege. Ensure that users have control over their data and can revoke permissions at any time.

Example requesting location permission:

```
import 'package:permission_handler/permission_handler.dart';

Future<void> requestLocationPermission() async {

final status = await Permission.location.request();

if (status.isGranted) {

// Location access granted, proceed with location-based functionality

} else if (status.isDenied) {

// Location access denied, inform the user

}

}
```

5. Privacy Policies and User Consent

Clearly communicate your app's privacy policy to users, and obtain their informed consent for data collection and processing. Ensure compliance with applicable privacy regulations, such as GDPR or CCPA.

6. Data Storage Compliance

If your app handles sensitive data, consider encrypting data at rest, using secure storage solutions, and complying with industry-specific data protection standards.

7. Regular Security Audits

Perform security audits and code reviews regularly to identify and mitigate vulnerabilities. Stay informed about security best practices and apply security patches promptly.

By following these practices, you can significantly enhance the security and privacy of your Flutter app, building trust with your users and protecting their sensitive information.

7.5. Offline Data Synchronization

Offline data synchronization is a crucial aspect of mobile app development, ensuring that your Flutter app remains functional even when the user's device is not connected to the internet. In this section, we will explore strategies and techniques for implementing offline data synchronization in your Flutter applications.

1. Why Offline Data Synchronization?

Offline data synchronization is essential for several reasons:

- **User Experience:** Users expect your app to work seamlessly, regardless of their internet connection status. Offline access enhances user experience and satisfaction.
- **Data Integrity:** Ensures that data remains consistent and up-to-date, even when the device is offline or experiences intermittent connectivity.

• **Reduced Latency:** Fetching data locally is faster than retrieving it from a remote server, leading to reduced latency and improved app responsiveness.

• **Increased Availability:** Your app can be used in remote areas or places with poor network coverage.

2. Caching and Local Storage

One of the primary techniques for offline data synchronization is caching data locally on the user's device. You can use packages like hive, sqflite, or moor to implement local data storage and retrieval efficiently.

Example using the hive package:

```
dependencies:

hive: ^2.0.4

hive_flutter: ^1.1.0

dev_dependencies:

hive_generator: ^1.1.0

build_runner: ^2.1.7

import 'package:hive/hive.dart';

void storeDataLocally() async {

final box = await Hive.openBox('my_data_box');

await box.put('key', 'value');

}
```

```
void retrieveDataLocally() async {
final box = await Hive.openBox('my_data_box');
final value = box.get('key');
print('Retrieved value: $value');
}
```

3. Background Data Sync

Implement background data synchronization to periodically fetch updates from the server, even when the app is not actively in use. Utilize packages like background_fetch or workmanager for background tasks.

Example using the background_fetch package:

```
dependencies:
background_fetch: ^0.9.6
dev_dependencies:
flutter_launcher_icons: ^0.10.0
import 'package:background_fetch/background_fetch.dart';
void configureBackgroundSync() {
BackgroundFetch.configure(
BackgroundFetchConfig(
minimumFetchInterval: 15, // Fetch data every 15 minutes
stopOnTerminate: false,
```

```
enableHeadless: true,
requiredNetworkType: NetworkType.CONNECTED,
),
(String taskId) async {
// Perform data synchronization here
BackgroundFetch.finish(taskId);
},
);
}
```

4. Conflict Resolution

When synchronizing data between the local and remote sources, conflicts may arise if data has been modified in both places. Implement conflict resolution strategies to ensure data consistency.

5. Offline Mode Handling

Provide a clear user interface that informs users when they are in offline mode and what features are available. Allow users to queue actions for synchronization when they regain connectivity.

6. Testing Offline Scenarios

Test your app thoroughly under various offline scenarios, including loss of connectivity during data synchronization. Use Flutter's testing libraries to simulate offline conditions and verify the app's behavior.

7. Error Handling and Recovery

Plan for error handling and recovery mechanisms in case of data synchronization failures. Implement retry mechanisms and provide clear error messages to users.

Offline data synchronization is a complex but critical aspect of mobile app development. By following these strategies and techniques, you can ensure that your Flutter app provides a seamless and reliable experience to users, regardless of their internet connection status.

Chapter 8: Integrating APIs and Third-Party Services

8.1. Consuming RESTful APIs

In this section, we will explore how to integrate RESTful APIs into your Flutter application. RESTful APIs are a common way to exchange data between your app and external services or databases. Flutter provides various packages and libraries to simplify the process of making HTTP requests and handling API responses.

1. HTTP Requests

To consume RESTful APIs, you'll often need to make HTTP requests, such as GET, POST, PUT, or DELETE. Flutter's http package is a popular choice for handling these requests.

dependencies:

http: ^0.13.3

Here's an example of making a GET request to retrieve data from an API:

import 'dart:convert';

import 'package:http/http.dart' as http;

Future fetchData() async {

final response = await http.get(Uri.parse('https://api.example.com/data'));

if (response.statusCode == 200) {

```
final data = json.decode(response.body);

// Process the data here

} else {

throw Exception('Failed to load data');

}

}
```

2. Handling API Responses

API responses are typically in JSON format. You can use the dart:convert library to parse JSON data into Dart objects. Make sure to handle errors and edge cases gracefully.

3. Authentication

Many APIs require authentication using tokens or API keys. You can pass authentication headers in your HTTP requests for secure access.

```
import 'package:http/http.dart' as http;

Future fetchDataWithAuthentication() async {

final headers = {

'Authorization': 'Bearer YOUR_ACCESS_TOKEN',

};

final response = await http.get(

Uri.parse('https://api.example.com/secure-data'),
```

```
headers: headers,
);
// Handle the response as needed
}
```

4. Error Handling

Always implement error handling for network requests. Consider using try-catch blocks to capture and handle exceptions. You can also create custom error classes for better error management.

5. Asynchronous Programming

API calls are typically asynchronous operations. Use async and await to work with API calls without blocking the main UI thread.

6. Using Dart Models

To represent data from APIs in a structured way, create Dart classes or models that mirror the JSON structure. You can then parse the JSON response into these models for easy manipulation.

7. Testing

Write unit tests and integration tests to ensure that your API integration works as expected. Use mock server responses for testing different scenarios.

8. Pagination and Data Fetching

For APIs that return large datasets, implement pagination to fetch data in smaller chunks. Use libraries like infinite_scroll_pagination to manage data efficiently.

9. Rate Limiting and Throttling

Respect rate limits imposed by APIs to avoid getting blocked. Implement rate limiting and throttling mechanisms in your app to prevent excessive API requests.

Integrating RESTful APIs is a fundamental part of building modern Flutter applications. With the right packages and best practices, you can fetch and manipulate data from external sources efficiently, enhancing the functionality of your app.

8.2. OAuth and Secure Authentication

In this section, we'll delve into OAuth and secure authentication in the context of integrating APIs and third-party services into your Flutter application. OAuth is a widely-used protocol for securely authorizing third-party applications to access resources on a user's behalf without exposing their credentials.

1. Understanding OAuth

OAuth (Open Authorization) is an authorization framework that allows applications to access user data from a resource server without exposing the user's credentials to the application. It is commonly used when integrating with services like social media platforms or cloud providers.

2. OAuth Flows

OAuth defines several flows, each designed for specific use cases:

- **Authorization Code Flow**: Suitable for web and mobile apps. It involves redirecting the user to an authorization server, obtaining an authorization code, and exchanging it for an access token.

- **Implicit Flow**: Primarily used in single-page applications (SPAs) and mobile apps where client-side JavaScript is involved. It directly returns the access token to the app.

- **Client Credentials Flow**: Typically used for machine-to-machine authentication, where there is no user involvement. It exchanges client credentials for an access token.

- **Resource Owner Password Credentials (ROPC) Flow**: Least recommended and should be avoided whenever possible. It involves collecting the user's credentials and exchanging them for an access token.

3. OAuth Packages for Flutter

To implement OAuth in your Flutter app, you can use packages like flutter_appauth or oauth2. These packages provide utilities for handling OAuth flows and securely managing tokens.

4. Registering Your App

Before implementing OAuth, you need to register your app with the service provider. This involves creating an application in their developer portal and obtaining client credentials (client ID and client secret).

5. Redirect URLs

OAuth flows often require redirect URLs to return the user to your app after authorization. Ensure that you handle these redirects properly in your Flutter app.

6. Storing Tokens Securely

Once you obtain access tokens, store them securely using packages like flutter_secure_storage to prevent unauthorized access.

```
import 'package:flutter_secure_storage/flutter_secure_storage.dart';

final storage = FlutterSecureStorage();

// Storing a token securely

await storage.write(key: 'access_token', value: 'your_access_token');

// Retrieving a token

final token = await storage.read(key: 'access_token');
```

7. Token Expiration and Refresh

Access tokens have a limited lifespan. Be prepared to handle token expiration by implementing token refresh flows when using long-lived access tokens.

8. User Consent

In OAuth, users must grant consent to the application before it can access their data. Handle user consent dialogs properly and explain why your app needs certain permissions.

9. Revoking Access

Users should have the ability to revoke an application's access to their data. Provide an option for users to disconnect their accounts from your app.

10. Testing OAuth Integration

Test various scenarios, including successful authentication, token refresh, and error handling. Mock server responses during testing to cover different cases.

OAuth is a powerful and secure way to integrate with third-party services and APIs in your Flutter app. Understanding the OAuth flows, securing tokens, and handling user consent are crucial aspects of implementing OAuth authentication successfully. Choose the appropriate OAuth flow based on your app's requirements and the service you are integrating with.

8.3. Payment Gateway Integration

In this section, we will explore payment gateway integration in your Flutter application. Payment gateways play a crucial role in e-commerce and various online services, allowing businesses to accept payments securely from customers. Integrating a payment gateway into your Flutter app requires careful consideration of security, user experience, and compliance with industry standards.

1. Choosing a Payment Gateway

The first step in payment gateway integration is selecting a suitable provider. Consider factors such as supported payment methods, transaction fees, international support, and the availability of an SDK or API for Flutter.

Some popular payment gateway providers for Flutter include Stripe, PayPal, Square, and Braintree.

2. Setting Up Your Merchant Account

Once you've chosen a payment gateway, you'll need to create a merchant account with the provider. This account enables you to receive payments and manage transactions. Be prepared to provide business information and bank details during the registration process.

3. Integrating the Payment Gateway SDK

Most payment gateways offer SDKs or APIs that you can use to integrate their services into your Flutter app. Depending on your chosen provider, you'll need to install the corresponding Flutter package and configure it with your credentials.

For example, when integrating Stripe, you can use the "stripe_payment" package:

```
import 'package:stripe_payment/stripe_payment.dart';

// Initialize the Stripe payment configuration

StripePayment.setOptions(

StripeOptions(

publishableKey: 'your_publishable_key',

merchantId: 'your_merchant_id',

),

);
```

4. Implementing Payment Flows

Payment gateway integration involves implementing payment flows in your app. Typical steps include:

- Collecting payment details from the user, such as credit card information or digital wallets.
- Sending a payment request to the gateway.
- Handling the response, which includes a transaction ID and status.
- Updating your app's UI based on the payment result.

Ensure that you follow best practices for security, such as encrypting sensitive data and complying with Payment Card Industry Data Security Standard (PCI DSS) requirements.

5. Handling Errors and Edge Cases

Payment gateway integration may encounter errors, declined transactions, or connectivity issues. Your app should gracefully handle these scenarios by providing clear error messages and options for users to retry or choose an alternative payment method.

6. Testing in a Sandbox Environment

Most payment gateways offer a sandbox or test environment that simulates real transactions without actual money changing hands. Use this environment for thorough testing to ensure your payment flow works correctly.

7. Securing Payment Data

Security is paramount in payment processing. Never store sensitive payment information on the device or server. Instead, use tokenization techniques provided by the payment gateway to securely handle transactions.

8. Compliance and Regulations

Be aware of legal and regulatory requirements for handling payments in your region and industry. Ensure that your app complies with data protection laws and financial regulations.

9. User Experience

A seamless and intuitive payment experience is essential for user satisfaction. Design your payment screens to be user-friendly, with clear instructions and visual cues.

10. Analytics and Reporting

Implement analytics to track payment transactions and monitor the performance of your payment gateway integration. This data can help you optimize the payment process and identify any issues.

11. Documentation and Support

Refer to the official documentation provided by your chosen payment gateway for detailed integration instructions and troubleshooting guidance. Additionally, consider leveraging community resources and forums for support and best practices.

Integrating a payment gateway into your Flutter app can open up revenue streams and enhance the user experience. However, it requires careful planning, attention to security, and compliance with industry standards. Choose a reliable payment gateway provider, follow best practices, and thoroughly test your payment flow to ensure smooth and secure transactions for your users.

8.4. Social Media Integration

Social media integration is a valuable feature that can enhance user engagement in your Flutter application. It allows users to connect their social media accounts, share content, and interact with your app through their favorite platforms. In this section, we'll explore how to integrate social media features into your Flutter app.

1. Choosing Social Media Platforms

Start by identifying which social media platforms are most relevant to your app's audience. Common options include Facebook, Twitter, Instagram, and LinkedIn. Each platform may offer different integration possibilities and features, so choose wisely.

2. Authentication and Authorization

To enable social media integration, you'll need to implement authentication and authorization. This involves allowing users to log in or connect their social media accounts to your app. You can use packages like flutter_facebook_auth for Facebook, twitter_login for Twitter, or google_sign_in for Google authentication.

Here's an example of using the flutter_facebook_auth package for Facebook authentication:

```
import 'package:flutter_facebook_auth/flutter_facebook_auth.dart';

// Log in with Facebook
```

```
try {
final LoginResult result = await FacebookAuth.instance.login();
if (result.status == LoginStatus.success) {
final AccessToken accessToken = result.accessToken!;
// Use the access token for further interactions with Facebook.
} else {
// Handle authentication failure.
}
} catch (e) {
// Handle exceptions.
}
```

3. Sharing Content

Once users are authenticated, you can enable them to share content from your app to their social media profiles. This can include sharing images, links, or text. Use the respective social media packages to implement sharing functionality.

For example, to share a link on Facebook using the flutter_facebook_share package:

```
import 'package:flutter_facebook_share/flutter_facebook_share.dart';
// Share a link on Facebook
await FacebookShare.share(
```

```
link: Uri.parse('https://example.com'),
);
```

4. Fetching User Data

Social media integration can also involve fetching user data, such as profile information and friends' lists. Make sure to request the necessary permissions from users and handle data securely and responsibly.

5. Real-time Updates

Some social media platforms offer real-time updates, allowing your app to receive notifications about user interactions or new content. Implementing real-time updates may require additional setup and integration with webhooks or APIs provided by the platforms.

6. Customization and Branding

Consider customizing the appearance and behavior of social media features to match your app's branding and user experience. This includes designing share buttons, profile views, and feed displays that align with your app's design guidelines.

7. Error Handling

Handle potential errors and exceptions gracefully when integrating with social media platforms. This includes scenarios like authentication failures, network issues, or rate limits imposed by the platforms.

8. Compliance with Platform Policies

Each social media platform has its policies and guidelines for integration. Ensure that your app complies with these policies to avoid any issues or restrictions. Failure to adhere to platform policies could lead to your app's suspension or removal from app stores.

9. Testing and Debugging

Thoroughly test social media integration in both development and production environments. Use test accounts provided by the social media platforms to simulate various scenarios and ensure that sharing, authentication, and other features work as expected.

10. User Privacy

Respect user privacy and permissions when accessing social media data. Clearly communicate to users what data your app will access and how it will be used. Implement mechanisms for users to revoke access to their social media accounts if needed.

11. User Engagement Strategies

Leverage social media integration to increase user engagement. Encourage users to share achievements, content, or invites with their social networks. Implement features like social login to streamline the onboarding process and boost user retention.

12. Documentation and Support

Refer to the official documentation provided by the social media platforms for detailed integration instructions, API references, and best practices. Additionally, stay informed about any updates or changes to the platforms' APIs and features.

Social media integration can enhance your Flutter app's reach and engagement by leveraging the power of social networks. Whether it's sharing content, authenticating users, or fetching data, careful planning and implementation are key to creating a seamless and user-friendly experience. Choose the social media platforms that align with your app's goals, follow best practices, and prioritize user privacy and security.

8.5. Using Firebase with Flutter

Firebase is a comprehensive platform provided by Google for building mobile and web applications. It offers a wide range of services that can be seamlessly integrated into your Flutter app. In this section, we'll explore how to use Firebase with Flutter to enhance your app's functionality.

1. Setting Up Firebase

Before you can use Firebase services in your Flutter app, you need to set up a Firebase project and configure it. Follow these steps:

1. Create a Firebase project on the Firebase Console (https://console.firebase.google.com/).
2. Add your Flutter app to the Firebase project by registering it with your app's package name.
3. Download the google-services.json file (for Android) or GoogleService-Info.plist file (for iOS) and place them in the respective directories of your Flutter app.
4. Configure your app to use Firebase by adding the Firebase SDK dependencies to your pubspec.yaml file.

Here's an example pubspec.yaml configuration for Firebase:

dependencies:

```
flutter:
sdk: flutter
firebase_core: ^latest_version
# Add other Firebase service dependencies as needed.
```

2. Firebase Authentication

Firebase Authentication provides secure and easy-to-implement authentication methods. You can integrate Firebase Authentication with Flutter to enable user registration, login, and management.

```
import 'package:firebase_auth/firebase_auth.dart';
// Register a user with email and password
Future<void> registerUser(String email, String password) async {
try {
await FirebaseAuth.instance.createUserWithEmailAndPassword(
email: email,
password: password,
);
} catch (e) {
// Handle registration errors.
}
}
// Sign in with email and password
```

```
Future<void> signInUser(String email, String password) async {
try {
await FirebaseAuth.instance.signInWithEmailAndPassword(
email: email,
password: password,
);
} catch (e) {
// Handle sign-in errors.
}
}
// Sign out
Future<void> signOutUser() async {
await FirebaseAuth.instance.signOut();
}
```

3. Firestore Database

Firestore is a NoSQL cloud database provided by Firebase. It allows you to store and sync data in real-time. You can use Firestore as your app's backend database.

```
import 'package:cloud_firestore/cloud_firestore.dart';
// Add a document to Firestore
Future<void> addDataToFirestore() async {
```

```
try {
await FirebaseFirestore.instance.collection('users').add({
'name': 'John Doe',
'email': 'johndoe@example.com',
});
} catch (e) {
// Handle Firestore errors.
}
}
// Query data from Firestore
Stream<QuerySnapshot> getUsers() {
return FirebaseFirestore.instance.collection('users').snapshots();
}
```

4. Firebase Cloud Messaging (FCM)

Firebase Cloud Messaging (FCM) allows you to send push notifications to your Flutter app's users. You can use FCM to engage users and keep them informed about updates and events.

```
import 'package:firebase_messaging/firebase_messaging.dart';
// Initialize Firebase Messaging
final FirebaseMessaging _firebaseMessaging = FirebaseMessaging();
// Subscribe to a topic
```

```
void subscribeToTopic(String topic) {
_firebaseMessaging.subscribeToTopic(topic);
}
// Receive and handle push notifications
void configureFirebaseMessaging() {
_firebaseMessaging.configure(
onMessage: (Map<String, dynamic> message) async {
// Handle incoming message.
},
onLaunch: (Map<String, dynamic> message) async {
// Handle when the app is launched from a terminated state.
},
onResume: (Map<String, dynamic> message) async {
// Handle when the app is resumed from the background.
},
);
}
```

5. Firebase Storage

Firebase Storage allows you to store and serve user-generated content, such as images and videos. You can use Firebase Storage to manage and serve media files in your Flutter app.

```
import 'package:firebase_storage/firebase_storage.dart';

// Upload a file to Firebase Storage

Future<void> uploadFileToStorage(String filePath) async {

try {

final Reference storageReference = FirebaseStorage.instance.ref().child('uploads/example.jpg');

await storageReference.putFile(File(filePath));

} catch (e) {

// Handle Firebase Storage errors.

}

}

// Retrieve a file from Firebase Storage

Future<String> getFileFromStorage() async {

try {

final Reference storageReference = FirebaseStorage.instance.ref().child('uploads/example.jpg');

final String downloadURL = await storageReference.getDownloadURL();

return downloadURL;

} catch (e) {

// Handle Firebase Storage errors.
```

```
return '';
}
}
```

6. Other Firebase Services

Firebase offers many other services, including Firebase Realtime Database, Firebase Hosting, Firebase Remote Config, and more. Explore these services based on your app's specific requirements and integrate them as needed.

Firebase is a powerful tool for building robust Flutter apps with features like authentication, real-time data synchronization, cloud storage, and push notifications. By following best practices and leveraging Firebase's capabilities, you can create a highly functional and engaging app for your users.

Chapter 9: Testing and Debugging

9.1. Writing Unit and Widget Tests

Testing is a crucial aspect of Flutter app development. It helps ensure that your app functions correctly, catches bugs early in the development process, and provides confidence in the code's reliability. In this section, we'll explore unit tests and widget tests, two fundamental testing approaches in Flutter.

1. Unit Tests

Unit tests focus on testing small, isolated parts (units) of your code, such as functions and classes, in isolation from the rest of the app. These tests verify that individual units of code behave as expected.

To write unit tests in Flutter, you can use the built-in testing framework provided by the test package.

Writing a Simple Unit Test

Here's an example of a unit test for a simple function:

```
// The function to be tested

int add(int a, int b) {

return a + b;

}

void main() {

test('Addition function test', () {
```

```
expect(add(2, 3), 5); // Expects the result to be 5
});
}
```

Running Unit Tests

You can run unit tests using the flutter test command from the terminal. Make sure your test files are located in a directory named test within your project.

2. Widget Tests

Widget tests focus on testing individual Flutter widgets and their interactions. These tests help ensure that the UI components render correctly and that user interactions produce the expected results.

Writing a Simple Widget Test

Here's an example of a widget test for a counter app:

```
import 'package:flutter_test/flutter_test.dart';
import 'package:my_app/counter.dart';
void main() {
testWidgets('Counter increments when the button is pressed', (WidgetTester tester) async {
// Build our app and trigger a frame.
await tester.pumpWidget(MyApp());
// Verify that our counter starts at 0.
```

```
expect(find.text('0'), findsOneWidget);

expect(find.text('1'), findsNothing);

// Tap the '+' icon and trigger a frame.

await tester.tap(find.byIcon(Icons.add));

await tester.pump();

// Verify that our counter has incremented.

expect(find.text('0'), findsNothing);

expect(find.text('1'), findsOneWidget);

});

}
```

Running Widget Tests

You can run widget tests using the flutter test command just like unit tests. Widget tests use the testWidgets function from the flutter_test package.

3. Mocking and Dependency Injection

In unit and widget tests, you may need to mock external dependencies or services, such as databases or network requests. Dependency injection is a common technique used to provide mock implementations of these dependencies during testing.

Flutter provides the mockito package for creating mock objects and provider for dependency injection.

```
// Example of mocking and dependency injection with provider
```

```
class MyService {
// Your service implementation
}
void main() {
test('Test something with mocked service', () {
final myServiceMock = MockMyService(); // Mocked service
final myProvider = Provider<MyService>(
create: (_) => myServiceMock,
);
// Use myProvider in your tests
});
}
```

4. Test Coverage

To measure the code coverage of your tests, you can use tools like flutter test—coverage and view the coverage report in the coverage/lcov-report directory. Code coverage helps identify areas of your code that are not covered by tests.

5. Continuous Integration (CI)

Integrating testing into your CI/CD pipeline is essential to ensure that tests are run automatically whenever changes are pushed to the repository. Popular CI/CD services like Travis CI, CircleCI, and GitHub Actions can be configured to run Flutter tests on different platforms.

6. Best Practices

- Write tests early in the development process.
- Maintain a balance between unit tests and widget tests.
- Ensure tests are reliable and not flaky.
- Test edge cases and potential error scenarios.
- Use mock objects for external dependencies.
- Automate test execution in CI/CD pipelines.

By following these testing practices, you can improve the quality of your Flutter apps, reduce the number of bugs, and enhance the overall user experience. Testing is an ongoing process, and regular test maintenance is essential as your app evolves.

9.2. Integration Testing in Flutter

Integration testing in Flutter is a higher-level testing approach that focuses on testing how different parts of your app work together as a whole. Unlike unit tests, which test isolated units of code, and widget tests, which test individual widgets, integration tests simulate user interactions and test the behavior of your app's user interface.

1. Writing Integration Tests

Integration tests are written in Dart and use the flutter_driver package to interact with your app as if a user were using it. These tests can cover scenarios such as navigating through screens, filling out forms, and verifying that data is displayed correctly.

Structure of an Integration Test

Here's an example of the basic structure of an integration test:

```
import 'package:flutter_driver/flutter_driver.dart';

import 'package:test/test.dart';

void main() {

group('My App Integration Test', () {

FlutterDriver driver;

// Connect to the Flutter app before running the tests.

setUpAll(() async {

driver = await FlutterDriver.connect();

});

// Close the connection to the app after the tests.

tearDownAll(() async {

if (driver != null) {

driver.close();

}

});

test('Test screen navigation', () async {

// Navigate to a specific screen.

await driver.tap(find.byValueKey('navigate_button'));
```

```
// Verify that we are on the expected screen.

expect(await driver.getText(find.byValueKey('screen_title')), 'Screen Title');

});

// Add more test cases as needed.

});

}
```

Running Integration Tests

To run integration tests, you need to use the flutter drive command. For example:

```
flutter drive—target=test_driver/app.dart
```

The test_driver/app.dart file should contain the entry point for your integration tests.

2. Widget Key

In integration tests, you often use keys to locate and interact with widgets. Keys are a way to uniquely identify widgets in your app's widget tree. You can assign a key to a widget using the Key class.

```
Widget build(BuildContext context) {

return MaterialApp(

home: Scaffold(

body: Center(
```

```
child: Text(
'Hello, World!',
key: Key('hello_text'), // Assign a key to the Text widget.
),
),
),
);
}
```

3. Interacting with Widgets

Integration tests use methods provided by flutter_driver to interact with widgets. Common interactions include tapping, entering text, and scrolling. For example:

```
// Tapping a widget with a specific key.
await driver.tap(find.byValueKey('my_button'));
// Entering text into a TextField.
await driver.enterText(find.byValueKey('text_field'), 'Hello');
// Scrolling a ListView.
await driver.scroll(find.byValueKey('list_view'), 0, -300, Duration(milliseconds: 500));
```

4. Testing on Real Devices and Emulators

Integration tests are typically run on real devices or emulators, making them more representative of how users will interact with your app. You can specify the target device using the —device-id flag when running integration tests.

5. Continuous Integration (CI) for Integration Tests

Integrating integration tests into your CI/CD pipeline is crucial for automated testing. Similar to unit and widget tests, you can configure CI services to run integration tests when changes are pushed to your repository. This ensures that your app's functionality remains intact throughout the development lifecycle.

6. Best Practices

- Write integration tests for critical user flows.
- Keep tests organized in groups and name them descriptively.
- Use keys to uniquely identify widgets.
- Ensure that your app's UI is stable before writing integration tests.
- Regularly update and maintain your integration tests as your app evolves.

Integration testing helps you catch issues related to the interaction between different parts of your app and provides confidence in the overall functionality of your Flutter app. When combined with unit and widget tests, integration tests contribute to a robust testing strategy for your Flutter project.

9.3. Debugging Techniques and Tools

Debugging is a critical part of the software development process. It involves identifying and fixing issues, errors, and unexpected behavior in your code. In Flutter development, debugging is equally important to ensure your app functions correctly and to enhance your productivity. This section explores various debugging techniques and tools available for Flutter developers.

1. Debugging in Flutter

Flutter provides several ways to debug your application, from simple print statements to powerful debugging tools. Here are some common debugging techniques in Flutter:

Print Statements

The simplest debugging method is using print statements to log information to the console. You can insert print statements in your code to track the flow of execution and inspect variable values.

```
void myFunction() {

print('Entering myFunction');

// ...

print('Exiting myFunction');

}
```

Logging Libraries

Flutter offers logging libraries like logger and flutter_bloc that provide more sophisticated logging capabilities. These libraries allow you to log different log levels, categorize logs, and configure log output.

```
import 'package:logger/logger.dart';

final logger = Logger();

void myFunction() {

logger.d('Entering myFunction');

// ...

logger.d('Exiting myFunction');

}
```

DevTools

Flutter DevTools is a powerful set of tools that helps you analyze and debug your Flutter apps. You can access DevTools by running the following command in your terminal:

```
flutter pub global run devtools
```

DevTools provides various tabs for inspecting your app's performance, memory usage, network requests, and more. It also offers a widget inspector for visualizing your app's widget tree.

2. Flutter Inspector

The Flutter Inspector is an invaluable tool for debugging and understanding your app's user interface. It is integrated into the Flutter DevTools suite and can be accessed from your browser when DevTools is running.

Key features of the Flutter Inspector include:

- **Widget Tree**: Visualize your app's widget tree and understand the hierarchy of widgets.

- **Interactive Debugging**: You can select widgets in the tree and inspect their properties and states.

- **Hot Reload**: Flutter's hot reload feature allows you to make code changes and see the results instantly in your app.

3. Debugging in IDEs

Most popular integrated development environments (IDEs) like Visual Studio Code (VS Code) and Android Studio offer built-in support for Flutter debugging. You can set breakpoints, inspect variables, and step through your code while running your app.

VS Code Debugging

To debug your Flutter app in VS Code, you can create a launch.json configuration file and specify the debugging settings. VS Code provides a visual debugger with features like stepping through code, inspecting variables, and watching expressions.

4. Logging and Error Handling

Effective logging and error handling are essential for debugging. When an error occurs, make sure to log relevant information, such as error messages and stack traces. Additionally, consider using Flutter's error handling mechanisms, like ErrorWidget and FlutterError.onError, to gracefully handle errors and provide meaningful feedback to users.

5. Third-Party Tools

In addition to built-in Flutter tools, you can use third-party tools like Sentry, Firebase Crashlytics, and Bugsnag for error reporting and monitoring in production apps. These tools help you identify and prioritize issues reported by users.

6. Continuous Integration and Testing

Integrating debugging into your continuous integration (CI) and testing pipelines is essential. Automated tests, including unit tests, widget tests, and integration tests, can help identify and prevent regressions. CI services like Travis CI, CircleCI, and GitHub Actions can be configured to run your tests automatically.

Debugging is an iterative process that requires patience and systematic problem-solving. With the right debugging techniques and tools, you can efficiently track down and resolve issues in your Flutter applications, leading to a more reliable and user-friendly product.

9.4. Performance Tuning and Optimization

Performance optimization is a crucial aspect of Flutter app development. Ensuring that your app runs smoothly and efficiently not only enhances the user experience but also conserves device resources. In this section, we'll explore various techniques and best practices for optimizing the performance of your Flutter apps.

1. Profiling Your App

Before optimizing your app's performance, it's essential to understand where the bottlenecks are. Profiling tools, such as

Flutter's built-in DevTools and third-party options like the Dart Observatory, can help you identify performance issues.

- **Flutter DevTools**: As mentioned earlier, Flutter DevTools provides a suite of performance profiling tools. You can use the "Performance" tab to record and analyze your app's performance metrics, including CPU and memory usage. Look for spikes and areas that consume excessive resources.

2. Reducing Widget Rebuilds

Flutter's widget-based architecture encourages the rebuilding of widgets when changes occur. While this is powerful for creating dynamic UIs, it can also lead to unnecessary widget rebuilds. Here are ways to reduce widget rebuilds:

- **Use const Widgets**: Marking widgets as const wherever possible ensures that they are only created once, reducing unnecessary rebuilds.

```
const MyWidget();
```

- **const Constructors**: When defining custom widgets, provide const constructors for them to allow for compile-time constant widgets.

```
class MyCustomWidget extends StatelessWidget {

const MyCustomWidget({Key? key}) : super(key: key);

// ...

}
```

3. State Management

Efficient state management can significantly impact your app's performance. Consider the following approaches:

- **Provider and Riverpod**: These state management libraries are known for their performance optimizations. They efficiently rebuild only the necessary parts of your UI when state changes.

```
final myNotifier = StateNotifierProvider<MyNotifier,
MyState>((ref) {

return MyNotifier();

});
```

4. Using the const Keyword

In Dart and Flutter, the const keyword is your ally for optimizing performance. When used correctly, it can help reduce memory allocations and improve app speed.

5. Code Splitting

Code splitting is a technique to load parts of your app's code on-demand. Flutter supports code splitting out of the box, allowing you to split your app into smaller, independently loadable modules. This can reduce initial load times and improve performance.

6. Image Optimization

Images often consume a significant amount of memory. Optimize your app's images by:

- **Using Compressed Formats**: Choose image formats like WebP, which offer better compression compared to PNG or JPEG.

```
Image.asset('assets/my_image.webp');
```

- **Lazy Loading**: Load images on-demand, especially when dealing with a large number of images.

```
Image.network('https://example.com/my_image.jpg');
```

7. Minimizing Network Requests

Excessive network requests can slow down your app. Implement caching strategies and minimize unnecessary requests. Consider using packages like Dio or http for efficient network communication.

8. Widget Lifecycle

Understand the lifecycle of widgets, such as initState, dispose, and build. Properly managing resources and cleaning up when widgets are no longer needed is crucial for performance.

```
@override

void dispose() {

// Clean up resources here

super.dispose();

}
```

9. Reducing Animations

While animations can enhance user experience, complex animations can be resource-intensive. Use animations judiciously and consider simplifying them or providing options to disable them in your app's settings.

10. Memory Management

Efficient memory management is essential for app performance. Use tools like Dart's memory profiler to identify and fix memory leaks. Dispose of resources when they are no longer needed to free up memory.

```
void dispose() {

_controller.dispose();

super.dispose();

}
```

11. Testing for Performance

Regularly test your app's performance on real devices. Flutter's flutter drive command allows you to run performance tests and monitor frame rates and memory usage. Address performance issues as they are identified.

Optimizing the performance of your Flutter app is an ongoing process. By using profiling tools, following best practices, and continuously testing and improving your app's performance, you can ensure a smooth and responsive user experience.

9.5. Continuous Integration and Deployment

Continuous Integration (CI) and Continuous Deployment (CD) are essential practices in modern software development that help ensure the quality, reliability, and timely delivery of software projects. In this section, we'll explore how to set up CI/CD pipelines for your Flutter projects, enabling automated testing, building, and deployment.

1. Introduction to CI/CD

Continuous Integration (CI) is the practice of frequently integrating code changes into a shared repository, where automated builds and tests are executed. Continuous Deployment (CD) goes a step further by automating the deployment of successful builds to various environments, including production.

2. Setting Up CI/CD for Flutter

To implement CI/CD for your Flutter project, follow these general steps:

a. Choose a CI/CD Service

There are several CI/CD services available, such as:

- **GitHub Actions**: Integrated with GitHub repositories.
- **GitLab CI/CD**: Integrated with GitLab repositories.
- **Travis CI**: A popular choice for open-source projects.
- **Jenkins**: A highly customizable, open-source CI/CD tool.

- **CircleCI**: Offers cloud-based CI/CD solutions.

Choose the one that best fits your project's needs and integrates with your version control system.

b. Create Configuration Files

You'll need to create configuration files that define your CI/CD pipeline. These files specify how your app should be built, tested, and deployed. For example:

- For GitHub Actions, create a .github/workflows/main.yml file.
- For GitLab CI/CD, create a .gitlab-ci.yml file.

Here's an example of a simple GitHub Actions workflow file for a Flutter project:

```
name: Flutter CI/CD

on:

push:

branches:

- main

jobs:

build:

name: Build and Test

runs-on: ubuntu-latest
```

```
steps:

- name: Checkout code

uses: actions/checkout@v2

- name: Setup Flutter

uses: subosito/flutter-action@v4

with:

flutter-version: '2.x'

- name: Install dependencies

run: flutter pub get

- name: Run tests

run: flutter test

- name: Build APK

run: flutter build apk—release
```

c. Configure Deployment

Depending on your project, you may need to configure deployment to various environments, such as staging and production. You can use environment-specific variables and scripts to handle this.

d. Integrating Testing

Automated testing is a critical part of CI/CD. Ensure that your CI pipeline includes unit tests, widget tests, and integration tests. You can use tools like flutter test and packages like flutter_driver for integration testing.

e. Notifications and Alerts

Set up notifications and alerts to receive notifications when CI/CD builds and deployments succeed or fail. This ensures that you can address issues promptly.

f. Monitor and Iterate

Once your CI/CD pipeline is set up, monitor it regularly. Analyze build and test results, check deployment status, and address any failures promptly. Iterate on your pipeline configuration to improve it continuously.

3. Benefits of CI/CD for Flutter

Implementing CI/CD for your Flutter project offers several benefits:

- **Automated Testing**: CI/CD pipelines automate the execution of tests, ensuring that code changes don't introduce regressions.
- **Consistent Builds**: CI/CD ensures that every build is created from the same source code, reducing inconsistencies.
- **Faster Feedback**: Developers receive immediate feedback on the impact of their code changes, allowing for quick bug fixes.

- **Efficient Deployment**: CD automates the deployment process, reducing the risk of human error and streamlining releases.

- **Scalability**: CI/CD pipelines can scale to handle projects of all sizes, from small apps to large enterprise applications.

- **Collaboration**: CI/CD encourages collaboration by making it easy to integrate code changes from multiple contributors.

4. Conclusion

Continuous Integration and Continuous Deployment are crucial practices for Flutter app development. They enable automation, testing, and efficient deployment, ensuring that your Flutter apps are of high quality and can be delivered to users quickly and reliably. By setting up CI/CD pipelines and integrating them into your development workflow, you can streamline your app development process and improve overall project efficiency.

Chapter 10: Building for iOS and Android

In this chapter, we'll explore the process of building Flutter apps for both iOS and Android platforms. Flutter's cross-platform nature allows developers to create apps that run on both major mobile platforms with a single codebase. We'll cover various aspects of platform-specific development, including adapting UI, handling permissions, and publishing your app on the App Store and Google Play.

10.1. Platform-Specific Code and Native Integration

Flutter provides a unified framework for building mobile apps, but there are cases where you may need to incorporate platform-specific code or access native functionalities. This section delves into how you can seamlessly integrate native code and features into your Flutter app.

1. Platform Channels

Flutter offers a mechanism called "platform channels" to facilitate communication between Dart code and platform-specific code written in languages like Swift, Objective-C, or Java. You can use platform channels to invoke native methods and access native APIs.

Here's a basic example of invoking a native method using platform channels:

```
import 'package:flutter/services.dart';

const platform = MethodChannel('my_channel');
```

```
Future<void> invokeNativeMethod() async {

try {

final result = await platform.invokeMethod('nativeMethod');

print('Received from native: $result');

} on PlatformException catch (e) {

print('Error: ${e.message}');

}

}
```

2. Platform-Specific Widgets

Sometimes, you may want to use platform-specific widgets or components to ensure your app adheres to platform design guidelines. Flutter allows you to conditionally use platform-specific widgets using the Platform.is* flags:

```
import 'package:flutter/material.dart';

import 'package:flutter/cupertino.dart';

Widget buildPlatformSpecificUI() {

if (Platform.isIOS) {

return CupertinoButton(

child: Text('iOS Button'),

onPressed: () {

// Handle iOS-specific action
```

```
},
);
} else if (Platform.isAndroid) {
return ElevatedButton(
child: Text('Android Button'),
onPressed: () {
// Handle Android-specific action
},
);
} else {
return Container(); // Fallback for other platforms
}
}
```

3. Accessing Platform-Specific Features

To access platform-specific features like device sensors, permissions, or system services, you can use plugins or packages provided by the Flutter community or create your own native code bridges.

For instance, to access device location, you can use the geolocator package:

```
import 'package:geolocator/geolocator.dart';
Future<void> fetchLocation() async {
```

```
final position = await Geolocator.getCurrentPosition();

print('Latitude: ${position.latitude}, Longitude: ${position.longitude}');

}
```

4. Platform-Specific Configuration

Each platform may have specific configuration requirements, such as adding icons, splash screens, or setting up app signing for Android and iOS. You'll need to follow platform-specific guidelines to configure your app correctly.

5. Testing on Real Devices

To ensure your app works as expected on both iOS and Android devices, it's crucial to test on real devices. You can use emulators and simulators for initial testing, but real devices provide the most accurate representation of how your app performs.

6. Handling Platform Differences

While Flutter abstracts many platform differences, you should be aware of potential variations in behavior, UI, and performance between iOS and Android. Always test thoroughly and consider adapting your app's user experience for each platform.

7. Conclusion

Building Flutter apps for iOS and Android is a powerful capability of the framework. By leveraging platform channels, platform-specific widgets, and plugins, you can integrate native features seamlessly. It's essential to follow platform-specific guidelines, thoroughly test on real devices, and adapt your app's behavior to provide a consistent and user-friendly experience on both platforms. With Flutter, you can efficiently target a broad audience on multiple platforms while maintaining code reusability.

10.2. Adapting UI for iOS and Android

Creating a cross-platform app with Flutter is convenient, but it's important to ensure that your app's user interface (UI) looks and behaves correctly on both iOS and Android. These platforms have distinct design guidelines and user expectations. In this section, we'll explore strategies for adapting your app's UI to provide a native-like experience on both iOS and Android.

1. Platform-Specific Widgets

Flutter offers platform-specific widgets to help you create UI components that match the design patterns of iOS and Android. You can use Cupertino widgets for iOS-style UI and Material widgets for Android-style UI.

For instance, you can use CupertinoNavigationBar for iOS and AppBar for Android to create platform-specific app bars:

```
import 'package:flutter/cupertino.dart';

import 'package:flutter/material.dart';

Widget buildPlatformSpecificAppBar() {

if (Platform.isIOS) {

return CupertinoNavigationBar(

middle: Text('iOS App'),

);
```

```
} else if (Platform.isAndroid) {
return AppBar(
title: Text('Android App'),
);
} else {
return Container(); // Fallback for other platforms
}
}
```

2. Design Consistency

Although Flutter abstracts many UI differences, it's essential to follow the design guidelines of each platform. For example, iOS typically uses a bottom tab bar for navigation, while Android prefers a navigation drawer or tabs at the top. Ensure that your app's navigation and layout align with these guidelines.

3. Icons and Typography

iOS and Android have their own sets of icons and typography styles. Flutter provides packages like cupertino_icons for iOS-style icons and google_fonts for custom typography. Use these packages to maintain a consistent look and feel.

```
import 'package:cupertino_icons/cupertino_icons.dart';
import 'package:google_fonts/google_fonts.dart';
Widget buildPlatformSpecificUI() {
return Column(
```

```
children: [
Icon(
Platform.isIOS ? CupertinoIcons.mail : Icons.email,
size: 48.0,
),
Text(
'Platform-specific Text',
style: Platform.isIOS
? GoogleFonts.sanFrancisco()
: TextStyle(fontFamily: 'Roboto'),
),
],
);
}
```

4. Testing on Real Devices

To ensure your app's UI adaptation is effective, testing on real iOS and Android devices is crucial. Emulators and simulators provide a good starting point, but real devices may reveal subtle differences that need attention.

5. Customizing Themes

Flutter's Theme class allows you to customize the overall look of your app. You can create different themes for iOS and Android using platform checks. This way, you can control aspects like colors, fonts, and animations separately for each platform.

```
final ThemeData iosTheme = ThemeData(

primarySwatch: Colors.blue,

fontFamily: 'San Francisco',

);

final ThemeData androidTheme = ThemeData(

primarySwatch: Colors.green,

fontFamily: 'Roboto',

);

ThemeData getPlatformSpecificTheme() {

return Platform.isIOS ? iosTheme : androidTheme;

}
```

6. User Feedback and Reviews

Encourage users to provide feedback and reviews on the App Store and Google Play. Feedback from users on each platform can help you identify and address specific issues related to UI and functionality.

7. Conclusion

Adapting your Flutter app's UI for iOS and Android is crucial for delivering a positive user experience. By using platform-specific widgets, following design guidelines, and customizing themes, you can create an app that feels native on both platforms. Remember to test on real devices and gather user feedback to continuously improve your app's cross-platform compatibility and user satisfaction.

10.3. Handling Permissions and Device Features

Flutter apps often require access to various device features and permissions, such as the camera, GPS, microphone, and storage. In this section, we'll explore how to handle permissions and utilize device features effectively in your cross-platform Flutter app.

1. Requesting Permissions

1.1. Using the permission_handler Package

To request permissions, you can use the permission_handler package. It simplifies the process of checking and requesting permissions for various features like camera, location, and microphone.

```
import 'package:permission_handler/permission_handler.dart';

Future<void> requestCameraPermission() async {

final status = await Permission.camera.request();

if (status.isGranted) {
```

```
// Permission granted, you can use the camera.

} else {

// Permission denied.

}

}
```

1.2. Handling Permission Denied

When a permission is denied, it's essential to provide clear explanations to the user and guide them to the device settings to grant the necessary permissions manually.

2. Accessing Device Features

2.1. Camera and Image Capture

To capture photos or videos, you can use the camera package. It provides APIs for accessing the device's camera and taking pictures or recording videos.

```
import 'package:camera/camera.dart';

Future<void> takePicture() async {

final cameras = await availableCameras();

final firstCamera = cameras.first;

final controller = CameraController(firstCamera, ResolutionPreset.medium);

await controller.initialize();
```

```
final XFile image = await controller.takePicture();

// Process the captured image.

}
```

2.2. GPS and Location Services

For location-based features, you can use the geolocator package to access the device's GPS and get location updates.

```
import 'package:geolocator/geolocator.dart';

Future<void> fetchCurrentLocation() async {

final Position position = await Geolocator.getCurrentPosition(

desiredAccuracy: LocationAccuracy.high,

);

// Use the position data.

}
```

2.3. Microphone and Audio Recording

To record audio or work with the device's microphone, you can use the audio_recorder package. It allows you to record audio and save it as files.

```
import 'package:audio_recorder/audio_recorder.dart';

Future<void> startRecording() async {

final recording = await AudioRecorder.start();
```

```
// Start recording audio.

}
```

2.4. Storage and File Handling

Accessing the device's storage and handling files can be done using Flutter's built-in path_provider package. It provides paths to commonly used directories, such as the app's documents and cache directories.

```
import 'package:path_provider/path_provider.dart';

Future<void> saveFile() async {

final directory = await getApplicationDocumentsDirectory();

final filePath = '${directory.path}/my_file.txt';

// Write or read files in the specified directory.

}
```

3. Platform-Specific Considerations

Remember that handling permissions and device features may have platform-specific differences. You should test your app thoroughly on both iOS and Android devices to ensure it works as expected.

4. Security and Privacy

When accessing sensitive data like user location, images, or audio recordings, prioritize user privacy and security. Ensure that you handle data securely and request only the necessary permissions to avoid overburdening users with excessive requests.

5. Conclusion

Handling permissions and device features is an integral part of developing a Flutter app. By using Flutter packages tailored for permissions and device access, you can create a seamless and secure user experience while making the most of the device's capabilities. Always consider the platform-specific nuances and prioritize user privacy when implementing these features in your app.

10.4. Publishing Your App on App Store and Google Play

Once you've developed your Flutter app, the next step is to publish it on the App Store (for iOS) and Google Play Store (for Android). This section will guide you through the process of preparing and submitting your app to these platforms.

1. App Store (iOS)

1.1. Apple Developer Program

Before you can publish your app on the App Store, you need to enroll in the Apple Developer Program. This program allows you to access the necessary tools and resources for iOS app development. Enrollment comes with an annual fee, so make sure to review the current pricing on Apple's website.

1.2. Xcode and Flutter

To prepare your Flutter app for iOS, you'll need Xcode, which is only available on macOS. Ensure that you have Xcode installed, as it's the primary development environment for iOS apps. You'll also need to set up your Flutter project for iOS by running flutter create . in your project directory.

1.3. App Configuration

In your Flutter project, configure the app's metadata and settings in the ios/Runner/Info.plist file. Update the CFBundleName, CFBundleIdentifier, and other relevant properties to match your app's details.

1.4. Icons and Launch Screens

Create the necessary app icons and launch screens for various iOS device sizes. Use the flutter_launcher_icons package to generate icons, and design your launch screens to meet Apple's design guidelines.

1.5. Testing and Debugging

Thoroughly test your app on real iOS devices and emulators. Address any issues or bugs, and ensure that your app follows Apple's App Store Review Guidelines.

1.6. App Store Connect

Create an App Store Connect account, where you can manage your app's listing, pricing, and distribution. Prepare screenshots, app descriptions, and promotional materials for your app's store listing.

1.7. App Submission

Submit your app for review on App Store Connect. Apple's review process may take some time, during which they'll evaluate your app's functionality, quality, and compliance with guidelines.

2. Google Play Store (Android)

2.1. Google Play Console

To publish your Flutter app on the Google Play Store, you need a Google Play Console account. Sign up for one and pay the one-time registration fee.

2.2. Flutter for Android

Flutter offers seamless Android app development. Ensure you have the Android SDK installed and your Flutter project configured for Android by running flutter create . in your project directory.

2.3. App Configuration

Update the android/app/build.gradle file in your Flutter project to set the applicationId, which is your app's unique identifier on the Play Store.

2.4. App Icons and Screenshots

Design app icons and take screenshots of your app for the Play Store listing. Use the flutter_launcher_icons package to generate icons, and create engaging screenshots that showcase your app's features.

2.5. Testing and Debugging

Test your app on various Android devices and emulators, addressing any compatibility issues or bugs. Ensure that your app meets Google's Play Store policies and guidelines.

2.6. Play Store Listing

Create a listing for your app on the Google Play Console. Add app details, screenshots, descriptions, and pricing information. Optimize your app's store listing for discoverability.

2.7. App Release

Prepare a release of your app on the Google Play Console. Choose your release tracks (e.g., alpha, beta, production), and submit your app for review. Google will check for policy compliance and functionality.

3. Maintenance and Updates

After your app is published, continue to monitor user feedback, fix bugs, and release updates to improve your app. Regularly update your app's content and features to keep users engaged.

4. Conclusion

Publishing your Flutter app on the App Store and Google Play Store is a rewarding accomplishment. It allows you to reach a global audience and provide value to users. Ensure that you follow the guidelines and best practices of both platforms to maintain a positive app store presence.

10.5. Maintaining and Updating Your App

Maintaining and updating your Flutter app is an ongoing process that is crucial for keeping your users engaged and satisfied. In this section, we'll explore best practices for app maintenance, handling updates, and ensuring the long-term success of your application.

1. User Feedback and Bug Reports

Listening to user feedback is essential for improving your app. Encourage users to provide feedback and report bugs through a user-friendly interface within the app. Set up communication channels like email or a support system to address user concerns promptly.

2. Monitoring App Performance

Utilize tools like Firebase Performance Monitoring or third-party services to monitor your app's performance. Keep an eye on app crashes, slow-loading screens, and other issues that may affect the user experience. Regularly analyze performance data and address bottlenecks.

```
// Example of using Firebase Performance Monitoring in Flutter

import 'package:firebase_performance/firebase_performance.dart';

final Performance performance = FirebasePerformance.instance;

void trackPerformance() {

final trace = performance.newTrace('my_custom_trace');

trace.start();

// Code to be tracked for performance
```

```
trace.stop();

}
```

3. Security Updates

Stay vigilant about security vulnerabilities. Stay informed about potential security threats and update third-party packages regularly. Patch vulnerabilities promptly and inform your users if any security issues affect them.

4. Feature Enhancements

Consider user feedback and market trends when planning new features or enhancements. Regularly release updates that add value to your app and provide a better user experience. Keep your app competitive by staying ahead of the curve.

5. Compatibility Updates

Keep your app compatible with the latest operating system versions (iOS and Android). Test your app on new OS releases and make necessary adjustments to ensure it runs smoothly. Address any compatibility issues promptly to avoid user frustration.

```
// Example of checking the platform version in Flutter

import 'package:flutter/services.dart';

void checkPlatformVersion() async {

try {

final platformVersion = await MethodChannel('platform_version').invokeMethod('getPlatformVersion');

print('Platform version: $platformVersion');
```

```
} catch (e) {
print('Error getting platform version: $e');
}
}
```

6. Regular Updates

Consistently release updates to your app, whether they are small bug fixes or major feature additions. Regular updates show users that your app is actively maintained and improves their trust in your brand.

7. App Store Optimization (ASO)

Continuously optimize your app store listing. Experiment with keywords, app descriptions, and screenshots to improve your app's discoverability. Monitor your app's visibility and ratings in app stores and make adjustments as needed.

8. Marketing and Promotion

Promote your app through various channels, including social media, email marketing, and partnerships. Create promotional campaigns for major updates to attract new users and re-engage existing ones.

9. User Engagement

Implement features that encourage user engagement, such as push notifications, in-app messages, and personalized content. Engaged users are more likely to continue using your app and recommend it to others.

10. User Data Privacy

Stay compliant with data privacy regulations and inform users about your data collection practices. Ensure that user data is handled securely and transparently. Address privacy concerns promptly to maintain user trust.

11. App Performance Optimization

Continuously optimize your app's performance by minimizing resource usage, reducing loading times, and optimizing network requests. Regularly review and refactor code to ensure efficiency.

12. Backup and Disaster Recovery

Implement backup and disaster recovery strategies to safeguard user data. Regularly back up essential data and have a plan in place to recover from unexpected events such as server failures or data breaches.

13. Community Engagement

Engage with your app's user community through forums, social media, or dedicated community platforms. Encourage users to share their experiences and insights, fostering a sense of belonging and loyalty.

14. User Education

Provide user guides, tutorials, and FAQs within the app to help users navigate and utilize its features effectively. Educated users are more likely to engage with your app and avoid frustration.

15. Conclusion

Maintaining and updating your Flutter app is a continuous journey that requires dedication and attention to detail. By addressing user feedback, staying updated with the latest trends, and ensuring the security and performance of your app, you can keep your users happy and your app successful in the long run. Regular updates and improvements are key to standing out in the competitive app market.

Chapter 11: Advanced UI Components

Section 11.1: Custom Widgets and Complex UIs

In Flutter, custom widgets play a pivotal role in crafting unique and intricate user interfaces. While the framework provides a rich set of built-in widgets, there are situations where you'll need to create your own custom widgets to achieve specific design requirements or encapsulate complex functionality. Custom widgets empower you to build reusable components that maintain a consistent look and behavior throughout your app. This section will explore the creation of custom widgets and demonstrate how to use them to compose complex UIs.

Creating Custom Widgets

Creating a custom widget in Flutter is a straightforward process. You'll typically extend the StatelessWidget or StatefulWidget class to define your widget's behavior and appearance. Here's a simple example of a custom MyButton widget that displays a stylized button:

```
class MyButton extends StatelessWidget {

final String label;
```

```
final VoidCallback onPressed;

MyButton({required this.label, required this.onPressed});

@override

Widget build(BuildContext context) {

return ElevatedButton(

onPressed: onPressed,

child: Text(label),

);

}

}
```

In this example, the MyButton widget takes two parameters: label and onPressed, which determine the button's text and the callback function to execute when pressed. It uses an ElevatedButton internally to render the button.

Composing Complex UIs

Custom widgets shine when you need to compose complex UIs from smaller, reusable components. Let's say you're building a weather app with a custom weather card widget:

```
class WeatherCard extends StatelessWidget {

final String location;

final String temperature;

final String condition;
```

```
WeatherCard({
required this.location,
required this.temperature,
required this.condition,
});
@override
Widget build(BuildContext context) {
return Card(
elevation: 4,
child: Padding(
padding: const EdgeInsets.all(16.0),
child: Column(
children: [
Text(location, style: TextStyle(fontSize: 24)),
SizedBox(height: 8),
Text(temperature, style: TextStyle(fontSize: 48)),
SizedBox(height: 8),
Text(condition, style: TextStyle(fontSize: 18)),
],
),
```

```
),
);
}
}
```

The WeatherCard widget takes location, temperature, and condition as parameters and displays them in a card-based format. By encapsulating this UI component in a custom widget, you can easily reuse it throughout your app and maintain a consistent weather card design.

Benefits of Custom Widgets

Using custom widgets offers several advantages:

- **Reusability**: Custom widgets can be used multiple times across different parts of your app, promoting code reusability.
- **Maintainability**: By encapsulating complex UI elements in custom widgets, you can enhance code maintainability and readability.
- **Consistency**: Custom widgets allow you to enforce a consistent look and feel, ensuring a uniform user experience.
- **Abstraction**: Custom widgets abstract underlying implementation details, making your codebase more modular and easier to update.

As you continue to develop Flutter apps, custom widgets will become an essential tool for building elegant and maintainable user interfaces.

Conclusion

Custom widgets are a fundamental aspect of Flutter development, enabling you to create unique and reusable UI components. In this section, we explored the creation of custom widgets and their role in composing complex user interfaces. As you gain more experience with Flutter, custom widgets will become an integral part of your toolkit for crafting beautiful and functional apps.

Section 11.2: Gesture Detection and Custom Animations

In Flutter, building engaging and interactive user interfaces often involves detecting gestures and creating custom animations. This section delves into gesture detection and custom animations, showcasing how to make your Flutter app respond to user touches, drags, and swipes while adding delightful animations to provide a rich user experience.

Detecting Gestures

Flutter provides a wide range of built-in gesture detectors, making it easy to recognize user interactions and respond accordingly. Here are some common gestures you can detect and handle in Flutter:

1. Tap Gesture

The GestureDetector widget with the onTap property allows you to detect single taps on a widget. For example, you can create a button that responds to taps:

```
GestureDetector(
onTap: () {
// Handle tap gesture
// e.g., navigate to a new screen or perform an action
},
child: Container(
width: 100,
height: 40,
color: Colors.blue,
child: Center(
child: Text('Tap Me', style: TextStyle(color: Colors.white)),
),
),
)
```

2. Swipe Gesture

For detecting swipe gestures, you can use the Dismissible widget or the Draggable widget. The Dismissible widget allows you to dismiss a widget by swiping it off the screen:

```
Dismissible(
key: Key('item_key'),
onDismissed: (direction) {
// Handle the swipe gesture
// e.g., remove the item from a list
},
child: ListTile(
title: Text('Swipe me'),
),
)
```

3. Long Press Gesture

The onLongPress property of GestureDetector detects long-press gestures. You can use this to trigger actions when a user long-presses a widget:

```
GestureDetector(
onLongPress: () {
// Handle long press gesture
```

```
// e.g., show a context menu
},
child: Container(
width: 100,
height: 40,
color: Colors.red,
child: Center(
child: Text('Long Press Me', style: TextStyle(color: Colors.white)),
),
),
)
```

Creating Custom Animations

Flutter offers powerful animation capabilities to breathe life into your UI. You can create custom animations using the Animation and AnimationController classes. Here's a basic example of how to animate a widget's opacity:

```
class OpacityAnimationExample extends StatefulWidget {
@override
_OpacityAnimationExampleState createState() => _OpacityAnimationExampleState();
}
```

```
class _OpacityAnimationExampleState extends State<OpacityAnimationExample>
with SingleTickerProviderStateMixin {
late AnimationController _controller;
late Animation<double> _opacityAnimation;
@override
void initState() {
super.initState();
_controller = AnimationController(
duration: Duration(seconds: 2),
vsync: this,
);
_opacityAnimation = Tween<double>(
begin: 0.0,
end: 1.0,
).animate(_controller);
_controller.forward();
}
@override
void dispose() {
_controller.dispose();
```

```
super.dispose();
}
@override
Widget build(BuildContext context) {
return FadeTransition(
opacity: _opacityAnimation,
child: Container(
width: 100,
height: 100,
color: Colors.blue,
),
);
}
}
```

In this example, we create an animation that fades in a blue container. The AnimationController controls the animation, and the FadeTransition widget is used to apply the opacity animation to the container.

Gesture and Animation Synergy

Combining gesture detection with custom animations can result in engaging user interactions. For instance, you can animate a widget's position or size in response to a swipe or drag gesture. Flutter's flexibility allows you to create interactive and visually appealing UIs limited only by your creativity.

In summary, this section introduced gesture detection and custom animations in Flutter. You learned how to detect common gestures and create custom animations to enhance user experiences in your Flutter apps. These tools are invaluable for building dynamic and interactive interfaces that captivate users.

Section 11.3: Implementing Advanced Navigation Patterns

In Flutter, navigation plays a crucial role in creating a smooth user experience. While basic navigation between screens is straightforward, more complex apps may require advanced navigation patterns. This section explores various advanced navigation techniques and patterns to help you build robust and user-friendly Flutter applications.

Tab-Based Navigation

Tab-based navigation is a popular choice for organizing content and providing quick access to different sections of an app. Flutter offers the TabBar and TabBarView widgets, along with the DefaultTabController, to implement tabbed navigation effortlessly.

Here's a simplified example of implementing tab-based navigation using the TabBar and TabBarView:

```
class TabNavigationExample extends StatelessWidget {

@override

Widget build(BuildContext context) {
```

```
return DefaultTabController(
length: 3, // Number of tabs
child: Scaffold(
appBar: AppBar(
title: Text('Tab Navigation Example'),
bottom: TabBar(
tabs: [
Tab(text: 'Tab 1'),
Tab(text: 'Tab 2'),
Tab(text: 'Tab 3'),
],
),
),
body: TabBarView(
children: [
// Content for Tab 1
Center(child: Text('Tab 1 Content')),
// Content for Tab 2
Center(child: Text('Tab 2 Content')),
// Content for Tab 3
```

```
Center(child: Text('Tab 3 Content')),
],
),
),
);
}
}
```

In this example, we use DefaultTabController to manage the tabs, and TabBar and TabBarView widgets to display the tabs and their corresponding content. You can customize the appearance and behavior of the tabs as needed.

Drawer and Side Menu Navigation

For apps with more extensive navigation needs, implementing a drawer or side menu is a common approach. Flutter provides the Drawer widget, which can be used in conjunction with the Scaffold to create a navigation drawer.

Here's a basic example of implementing a drawer navigation pattern:

```
class DrawerNavigationExample extends StatelessWidget {
@override
Widget build(BuildContext context) {
return Scaffold(
appBar: AppBar(
```

```
title: Text('Drawer Navigation Example'),
),
drawer: Drawer(
child: ListView(
children: [
DrawerHeader(
child: Text('App Menu'),
decoration: BoxDecoration(
color: Colors.blue,
),
),
ListTile(
title: Text('Item 1'),
onTap: () {
// Handle navigation for Item 1
},
),
ListTile(
title: Text('Item 2'),
onTap: () {
```

```
// Handle navigation for Item 2
},
),
// Add more list items for navigation options
],
),
),
body: Center(child: Text('Main Content')),
);
}
}
```

In this example, the Drawer widget contains a list of items that users can tap to navigate to different sections of the app. You can customize the drawer's appearance and functionality to meet your app's requirements.

Bottom Navigation Bar

Bottom navigation bars are commonly used in mobile apps to switch between primary app sections. Flutter provides the BottomNavigationBar widget for implementing this navigation pattern.

Here's a simplified example of bottom navigation:

```
class BottomNavigationBarExample extends StatefulWidget {
```

```
@override
_BottomNavigationBarExampleState createState() => _BottomNavigationBarExampleState();

}

class _BottomNavigationBarExampleState extends State<BottomNavigationBarExample> {

int _currentIndex = 0;

@override

Widget build(BuildContext context) {

return Scaffold(

appBar: AppBar(

title: Text('Bottom Navigation Example'),

),

body: Center(child: Text('Page ${_currentIndex + 1}')),

bottomNavigationBar: BottomNavigationBar(

currentIndex: _currentIndex,

onTap: (index) {

setState(() {

_currentIndex = index;

});

},
```

```
items: [
BottomNavigationBarItem(
icon: Icon(Icons.home),
label: 'Home',
),
BottomNavigationBarItem(
icon: Icon(Icons.search),
label: 'Search',
),
BottomNavigationBarItem(
icon: Icon(Icons.favorite),
label: 'Favorites',
),
],
),
);
}
}
```

In this example, the BottomNavigationBar allows users to switch between three pages. The _currentIndex variable keeps track of the current page index.

Nested Navigation

In more complex apps, you may encounter scenarios where you need nested navigation, such as tabbed navigation within a drawer-based layout or vice versa. Flutter supports nesting navigation patterns, allowing you to combine various navigation techniques to create sophisticated user interfaces.

To implement nested navigation, you can use a combination of Navigator widgets within different sections of your app. Each Navigator maintains its navigation stack independently.

```
class NestedNavigationExample extends StatelessWidget {

@override

Widget build(BuildContext context) {

return MaterialApp(

home: Scaffold(

appBar: AppBar(

title: Text('Nested Navigation Example'),

),

drawer: Drawer(

// Drawer navigation content

),

body: Row(

children: [
```

```
// Side menu navigation content
Drawer(
// Side menu navigation
```

Section 11.4: Canvas and Custom Paint Techniques

Flutter provides a powerful way to create custom graphics and drawings using the CustomPaint widget and the underlying Canvas API. This section delves into canvas and custom paint techniques, allowing you to create intricate and visually appealing custom UI elements and visualizations.

Introduction to Custom Paint

The CustomPaint widget in Flutter allows you to draw custom graphics by providing a CustomPainter. A CustomPainter is responsible for defining how to paint on the canvas. This powerful feature enables you to create custom shapes, charts, animations, and more.

Here's a simplified example of using CustomPaint:

```
class CustomPaintExample extends StatelessWidget {
@override
Widget build(BuildContext context) {
return CustomPaint(
size: Size(200, 200),
painter: MyCustomPainter(),
```

```
);
}
}
class MyCustomPainter extends CustomPainter {
@override
void paint(Canvas canvas, Size size) {
final paint = Paint()
..color = Colors.blue
..strokeWidth = 2
..style = PaintingStyle.fill;
canvas.drawCircle(Offset(100, 100), 50, paint);
}
@override
bool shouldRepaint(CustomPainter oldDelegate) => false;
}
```

In this example, we create a custom circular shape using CustomPaint and a custom painter (MyCustomPainter). The paint method is responsible for drawing the circle on the canvas.

Drawing Paths and Lines

Beyond simple shapes, you can draw complex paths and lines using the Path class. This allows you to create custom shapes and paths for your UI elements.

```
class PathDrawingExample extends StatelessWidget {
@override
Widget build(BuildContext context) {
return CustomPaint(
size: Size(200, 200),
painter: MyPathPainter(),
);
}
}
class MyPathPainter extends CustomPainter {
@override
void paint(Canvas canvas, Size size) {
final paint = Paint()
..color = Colors.green
..strokeWidth = 3
..style = PaintingStyle.stroke;
final path = Path()
..moveTo(10, 10)
..lineTo(50, 50)
..lineTo(150, 50)
```

```
..close(); // Close the path to form a triangle

canvas.drawPath(path, paint);

}

@override

bool shouldRepaint(CustomPainter oldDelegate) => false;

}
```

In this example, we create a custom triangle shape using the Path class and draw it on the canvas.

Gradient and Shader Brushes

You can use gradients and shader brushes to apply advanced color effects to your custom drawings. Flutter provides various gradient types, including linear gradients, radial gradients, and sweep gradients.

```
class GradientExample extends StatelessWidget {

@override

Widget build(BuildContext context) {

return CustomPaint(

size: Size(200, 200),

painter: MyGradientPainter(),

);

}

}
```

```
class MyGradientPainter extends CustomPainter {
@override
void paint(Canvas canvas, Size size) {
final rect = Rect.fromPoints(Offset(10, 10), Offset(190, 190));
final gradient = LinearGradient(
colors: [Colors.red, Colors.blue],
begin: Alignment.topLeft,
end: Alignment.bottomRight,
);
final paint = Paint()
..shader = gradient.createShader(rect)
..style = PaintingStyle.fill;
canvas.drawRect(rect, paint);
}
@override
bool shouldRepaint(CustomPainter oldDelegate) => false;
}
```

In this example, we use a linear gradient to fill a rectangle with a smooth color transition from red to blue.

Custom Animation with CustomPainter

You can also leverage the CustomPainter class for custom animations. By updating the properties of your custom painter within a setState call, you can trigger repaints and achieve animations.

```
class AnimatedCustomPainterExample extends StatefulWidget {

@override

_AnimatedCustomPainterExampleState createState() => _AnimatedCustomPainterExampleState();

}

class _AnimatedCustomPainterExampleState extends State<AnimatedCustomPainterExample> {

double progress = 0.0;

@override

Widget build(BuildContext context) {

return GestureDetector(

onTap: () {

setState(() {

progress = (progress + 0.1).clamp(0.0, 1.0);

});

},

child: CustomPaint(
```

```
size: Size(200, 200),
painter: AnimatedCirclePainter(progress),
),
);
}
}
class AnimatedCirclePainter extends CustomPainter {
final double progress;
AnimatedCirclePainter(this.progress);
@override
void paint(Canvas canvas, Size size) {
final paint = Paint()
..color = Colors.blue
..strokeWidth = 5
..style = PaintingStyle.stroke;
final center = size.center(Offset.zero);
final radius = size.width / 2;
final sweepAngle = 360 * progress;
canvas.drawArc(
Rect.fromCircle(center: center,
```

Section 11.5: Creating 3D Effects in Flutter

Flutter primarily operates in a 2D rendering environment, but you can create stunning 3D effects and animations by leveraging various techniques and packages. This section explores methods for achieving 3D-like effects within your Flutter applications.

Perspective Transformations

One way to create a 3D-like effect is by applying perspective transformations to your widgets. Flutter provides the Transform widget, which allows you to apply 2D transformations, including translations, rotations, and scales. By combining these transformations cleverly, you can simulate 3D perspectives.

Here's a simplified example of applying perspective transformation to a widget:

```
Transform(

alignment: Alignment.center,

transform: Matrix4.identity()

..setEntry(3, 2, 0.002) // Perspective effect

..rotateX(0.1) // Rotate around X-axis

..rotateY(0.1), // Rotate around Y-axis

child: Container(

color: Colors.blue,

width: 100,

height: 100,
```

```
child: Center(

child: Text('3D-Like Effect'),

),

),

)
```

In this example, the Transform widget applies a combination of transformations to the child Container, resulting in a 3D-like appearance. Adjusting the rotation angles and perspective values allows you to achieve different effects.

Using Packages for 3D Effects

To create more advanced 3D effects, you can utilize packages like flutter_3d_obj and flutter_cube. These packages provide tools and widgets for rendering 3D models and scenes within your Flutter app.

Here's a basic example using the flutter_3d_obj package to render a 3D model:

```
import 'package:flutter/material.dart';

import 'package:flutter_3d_obj/flutter_3d_obj.dart';

class ThreeDModelViewer extends StatelessWidget {

@override

Widget build(BuildContext context) {

return Scaffold(

appBar: AppBar(
```

```
title: Text('3D Model Viewer'),
),
body: Center(
child: Container(
width: 300,
height: 300,
child: Object3D(
size: Size(300, 300),
path: 'assets/3d_model.obj',
asset: true,
zoom: 80,
),
),
),
);
}
}
```

In this example, we use the flutter_3d_obj package to load and display a 3D model from an OBJ file. You can customize the appearance and behavior of the 3D model using various parameters provided by the package.

Creating 3D-Like Transitions

Flutter's animation capabilities, such as Hero animations and custom route transitions, can be harnessed to create 3D-like transitions between screens. These transitions can provide a sense of depth and realism to your app's user interface.

For example, you can use the Hero widget to smoothly transition an image from one screen to another with a scaling effect, giving the illusion of depth. Additionally, you can implement custom page transitions that simulate 3D rotations or flips.

```
class FirstScreen extends StatelessWidget {

@override

Widget build(BuildContext context) {

return Scaffold(

appBar: AppBar(title: Text('First Screen')),

body: GestureDetector(

onTap: () {

Navigator.of(context).push(PageRouteBuilder(

pageBuilder: (context, animation, secondaryAnimation) {

return SecondScreen();

},

transitionsBuilder: (context, animation, secondaryAnimation, child) {

const begin = Offset(1.0, 0.0);
```

```
const end = Offset.zero;

const curve = Curves.easeInOut;

var tween = Tween(begin: begin, end: end).chain(CurveTween(curve: curve));

var offsetAnimation = animation.drive(tween);

return SlideTransition(position: offsetAnimation, child: child);

},

));

},

child: Hero(

tag: 'imageHero',

child: Image.asset('assets/sample_image.jpg'),

),

),

);

}

}

class SecondScreen extends StatelessWidget {

@override

Widget build(BuildContext context) {

return Scaffold(
```

```
appBar: AppBar(title: Text('Second Screen')),
body: GestureDetector(
onTap: () {
Navigator.of(context).pop();
},
child: Hero(
tag: 'imageHero',
child: Image.asset('assets/sample_image.jpg'),
),
),
);
}
}
```

In this example, we use the Hero widget to create a smooth image transition between the first and second screens. Additionally, a custom page transition is applied to achieve a 3D-like sliding effect when navigating between screens.

Experimenting with 3D-Like UI Elements

To add depth and realism to your Flutter app, consider experimenting with shadow effects, gradients, and layering of widgets. These techniques can simulate 3D lighting and material properties, enhancing the overall visual experience.

By combining perspective transformations, 3D model rendering, custom transitions, and creative UI design, you can create impressive 3D-like effects and interactions within your Flutter application, providing a unique and engaging user experience.

Chapter 12: Flutter for Web and Desktop

Section 12.1: Adapting Flutter Apps for Web

As Flutter continues to evolve, it extends its reach beyond mobile platforms to enable the creation of web and desktop applications. In this section, we'll explore how to adapt Flutter apps for web deployment and the key considerations when targeting web browsers.

Flutter Web Overview

Flutter's web support allows you to run your Flutter applications in modern web browsers, providing a consistent user experience across multiple platforms. This enables you to share a single codebase between your mobile and web applications, reducing development effort and maintenance.

To get started with Flutter for web, you'll need to follow these steps:

1. **Set Up Your Environment**: Ensure you have Flutter installed and up to date. You may need to enable web support by running flutter config—enable-web.
2. **Create a Web Project**: Use the flutter create command to generate a new Flutter project or migrate an existing one to web support.
3. **Run on the Web**: You can launch your Flutter web app using the flutter run -d web command, which starts a

development server and opens the app in your default web browser.

Web-Specific Considerations

While Flutter for web provides a powerful way to target the web, there are some web-specific considerations to keep in mind:

- **Responsive Design**: Web applications should adapt to various screen sizes and orientations. Flutter's LayoutBuilder and MediaQuery can help create responsive layouts that adjust to different screen dimensions.

- **Browser Compatibility**: Ensure your web app works well across different web browsers by testing it on popular ones like Chrome, Firefox, and Safari. Address any browser-specific issues that may arise.

- **Performance Optimization**: Web apps have different performance characteristics than mobile apps. Pay attention to web-specific performance optimizations, such as lazy loading assets and minimizing network requests.

- **Routing**: Implement client-side routing to enable deep linking and improve the user experience. Packages like fluro and router can help manage routing in your Flutter web app.

Handling Assets

In Flutter for web, assets such as images, fonts, and other resources are served over HTTP. You should specify these assets in your pubspec.yaml file and use them in your code as you would for mobile apps.

```
flutter:

assets:

- images/

- fonts/

Image.asset('images/logo.png')
```

Browser Debugging Tools

Web development often involves debugging in web browsers. Flutter for web supports debugging in popular browsers like Chrome and Firefox. You can use browser developer tools to inspect and debug your Flutter web app, set breakpoints, and view console logs.

Deployment

When deploying a Flutter web app, you can host it on various platforms, including static web hosting services like Netlify, Vercel, GitHub Pages, or your own web server. Ensure proper configuration and set up for your chosen hosting platform.

In summary, Flutter's web support allows you to leverage your existing Flutter knowledge to create web applications. With proper consideration for web-specific factors, you can build versatile apps that run seamlessly on both mobile devices and web browsers, expanding your app's reach and accessibility.

Section 12.2: Building Desktop Applications with Flutter

Flutter's versatility extends not only to web applications but also to desktop platforms, including Windows, macOS, and Linux. In this section, we'll explore how to use Flutter to build desktop applications and the key considerations for desktop development.

Desktop Support Overview

Flutter's desktop support is an evolving feature that allows developers to create native desktop applications using the same codebase as their mobile and web apps. Currently, Flutter offers stable support for Windows, macOS, and Linux, making it a compelling choice for cross-platform desktop development.

To get started with Flutter desktop development, follow these steps:

1. **Install Flutter**: Ensure you have Flutter installed and updated to the latest version.
2. **Enable Desktop Support**: You can enable desktop support for your Flutter project by running flutter config—enable-macos-desktop, flutter config—enable-windows-desktop, or flutter config—enable-linux-desktop depending on your target platform.
3. **Create a Desktop Project**: Use the flutter create command to generate a new Flutter project with desktop support, or add desktop support to an existing Flutter project.
4. **Run on Desktop**: To run your Flutter desktop app, use the

flutter run command followed by -d macos, -d windows, or -d linux to specify your target platform.

Platform-Specific Considerations

When developing desktop applications with Flutter, it's important to consider platform-specific guidelines and design principles. Each desktop platform has its own user interface conventions, and adhering to them will result in a more native and intuitive user experience.

- **macOS**: Follow macOS's Human Interface Guidelines (HIG) to create an app that integrates seamlessly with the macOS ecosystem. Use native macOS widgets and components for a native look and feel.

- **Windows**: Adhere to the Windows Desktop Guidelines to ensure your app follows Windows design principles. Use native Windows controls and styles for a consistent Windows experience.

- **Linux**: Linux desktop environments vary, so consider designing your app to be flexible and customizable. Use Linux-compatible UI libraries and themes where possible.

Plugins and Packages

Flutter's desktop support comes with a growing ecosystem of plugins and packages that enable you to access platform-specific features and functionalities. You can find packages for file system access, system tray integration, and more, making it easier to build desktop apps with rich capabilities.

Desktop Debugging

Debugging Flutter desktop apps is similar to debugging mobile apps. You can use the Dart DevTools and Flutter DevTools browser-based tools for debugging and profiling your desktop app. Additionally, many desktop IDEs like Visual Studio Code offer excellent Flutter desktop debugging support.

Deployment

When it comes to deploying Flutter desktop apps, consider the distribution channels and platforms specific to each desktop operating system. On macOS, you can distribute your app through the Mac App Store or as a standalone package. On Windows, you can create installer packages, and on Linux, you can distribute your app through package managers or as a standalone executable.

In conclusion, Flutter's desktop support empowers developers to create cross-platform desktop applications with a single codebase. By understanding the platform-specific guidelines, leveraging available plugins and packages, and mastering debugging and deployment techniques, you can build native-quality desktop apps that reach a broader audience across different desktop operating systems.

Section 12.3: Cross-Platform Considerations

Developing desktop applications with Flutter introduces unique cross-platform considerations that are essential for a successful project. In this section, we'll delve into these important aspects to ensure your desktop app works seamlessly across different operating systems.

Platform-Specific Code

While Flutter provides a unified codebase for desktop, mobile, and web platforms, there may be cases where you need to write platform-specific code to accommodate variations between operating systems. Flutter offers mechanisms for platform-specific code execution through plugins and platform channels.

- **Plugins**: Flutter plugins are packages that provide access to platform-specific features. You can use existing plugins or create your own to interact with desktop-specific APIs. Plugins help keep platform-specific code separate and manageable.

- **Platform Channels**: Flutter's platform channel mechanism allows communication between Dart code and native platform code. You can invoke platform methods and pass data back and forth, enabling you to handle platform-specific tasks when necessary.

User Interface Design

Designing a user interface (UI) that adapts well to different desktop platforms is crucial for a consistent and native user experience. Consider the following UI design principles:

- **Platform-Specific Styling**: Apply platform-specific styles and design guidelines. For example, use native macOS widgets and adhere to the Windows Desktop Guidelines on Windows.

- **Layout Flexibility**: Design your UI to accommodate variations in screen sizes, resolutions, and aspect ratios across desktop platforms. Flutter's layout widgets, such as MediaQuery and Flexible, can help with responsive design.

- **Font and Text Scaling**: Ensure that text is legible and scaled appropriately for different desktop screen configurations. Flutter provides tools for responsive font and text scaling.

Testing on Multiple Platforms

To ensure your Flutter desktop app works correctly on different operating systems, you should test it on each target platform:

- **macOS**: Test your app on macOS to verify that it follows macOS's design principles, integrates with system features, and functions smoothly.

- **Windows**: Similarly, test your app on Windows to validate its adherence to Windows design guidelines and user expectations.

- **Linux**: Linux desktop environments can vary significantly. Consider testing on popular Linux distributions to ensure compatibility and functionality.

Use virtual machines or physical devices running each target operating system for comprehensive testing.

Continuous Integration (CI)

Implementing a CI/CD (Continuous Integration/Continuous Deployment) pipeline that includes automated testing on different desktop platforms is essential. Services like GitHub Actions, Travis CI, or GitLab CI can help automate the testing and deployment process, ensuring that your app remains consistent and bug-free across platforms.

Documentation

Clearly document any platform-specific code, configurations, and considerations in your project's documentation. This documentation will be valuable for you and your team members when maintaining and updating the app in the future.

Community and User Feedback

Leverage the.Flutter community and gather user feedback to identify platform-specific issues or user experience improvements. Community contributions and discussions can provide insights into cross-platform challenges and solutions.

In summary, developing cross-platform desktop applications with Flutter requires careful consideration of platform-specific code, user interface design, testing on multiple platforms, CI/CD integration, documentation, and community collaboration. By addressing these cross-platform considerations, you can create desktop apps that offer a consistent and native experience on macOS, Windows, and Linux.

Section 12.4: Performance Optimization for Web and Desktop

Optimizing performance is crucial when developing Flutter apps for web and desktop platforms. This section explores various strategies and techniques to ensure your app runs smoothly and efficiently on these platforms.

Minimizing Resource Usage

Both web and desktop environments have limited system resources compared to mobile devices. To ensure your app performs well, follow these resource optimization practices:

- **Memory Management**: Efficiently manage memory by avoiding memory leaks and unnecessary object creation. Use Dart's garbage collection and dispose of resources properly.

- **Asset Optimization**: Compress and optimize images, fonts, and other assets to reduce file sizes. Use formats and resolutions appropriate for desktop and web platforms.

- **Code Splitting**: Split your code into smaller modules to enable lazy loading. This reduces the initial load time and memory usage, as only necessary parts of your app are loaded on demand.

Responsive Design

Desktop platforms, in particular, come in various screen sizes and resolutions. To accommodate this diversity, adopt responsive design principles:

- **Layout Flexibility**: Use Flutter's layout widgets like MediaQuery and Flexible to create responsive UIs that adapt to different screen sizes and orientations.

- **Font Scaling**: Ensure that fonts and text are appropriately scaled to maintain readability across various screen configurations.

Hardware Acceleration

Leverage hardware acceleration when available to improve graphics and animations performance:

- **Graphics Hardware**: Flutter can use the GPU (Graphics Processing Unit) for rendering when possible. Utilize the RepaintBoundary widget to indicate areas that can be cached and rendered using GPU acceleration.

- **Animation Hardware**: Use Flutter's animation framework and Flutter's AnimatedContainer, Hero widgets, and more to take advantage of GPU-accelerated animations.

Profiling and Debugging

Efficiently identify and resolve performance bottlenecks by using profiling and debugging tools:

- **Dart DevTools**: Flutter's DevTools suite includes profiling tools to analyze your app's performance. Use them to identify areas that need optimization.

- **Chrome DevTools**: When developing for the web, Chrome DevTools provides in-depth profiling and debugging capabilities for web-based Flutter apps.

Code Splitting

Split your code into smaller modules and use code splitting to load only the necessary parts of your app on-demand. This reduces initial load times and memory usage, improving the overall performance.

```
import 'package:my_module/my_module.dart' deferred as myModule;

// Load the module when needed

loadMyModule() async {

await myModule.loadLibrary();

myModule.doSomething();

}
```

AOT Compilation (Ahead-of-Time)

For web and desktop deployments, consider using Ahead-of-Time (AOT) compilation. AOT compilation reduces runtime overhead and improves startup performance.

```
flutter build web—release
```

For desktop, use the —release flag when building your app to enable AOT compilation.

Optimized Asset Loading

When working with assets like images and fonts, ensure they are optimized for web and desktop platforms. Compress images and use appropriate formats to minimize file sizes.

Network Optimization

For web and desktop apps, network performance is critical. Optimize network requests by using HTTP/2, caching, and minimizing unnecessary requests.

```
import 'package:http/http.dart' as http;

void fetchData() async {

final response = await http.get('https://api.example.com/data');

if (response.statusCode == 200) {

// Process the data

} else {

// Handle error

}

}
```

Continuous Performance Testing

Implement continuous performance testing as part of your CI/CD pipeline. Automate performance tests to catch regressions and monitor your app's performance over time.

In conclusion, optimizing Flutter apps for web and desktop platforms requires careful consideration of resource usage, responsive design, hardware acceleration, profiling, debugging, and code splitting. By following these best practices, you can ensure that your app delivers a smooth and efficient user experience on a variety of desktop and web environments.

Section 12.5: Deploying Web and Desktop Applications

Deploying Flutter applications for web and desktop involves specific steps and considerations. This section provides guidance on how to package and distribute your Flutter apps effectively to reach your target audience on these platforms.

Web Deployment

To deploy a Flutter web app, follow these steps:

1. **Build Your App**: Generate optimized production-ready web code by running flutter build web—release.
2. **Hosting**: Choose a hosting service for your web app. Options include popular platforms like Netlify, Vercel, Firebase Hosting, GitHub Pages, or your own web server.
3. **Upload Files**: Upload the contents of the build/web directory to your hosting service. Ensure you deploy the index.html file and the entire assets directory along with your JavaScript and CSS files.
4. **Configure Routing**: If your web app uses client-side routing (e.g., navigation to different pages), make sure your hosting service supports URL rewriting for Flutter's HTML5 URLs.
5. **Set Up Domain**: Configure a custom domain or subdomain for your web app, if desired, and update DNS settings accordingly.
6. **Testing**: Test your deployed web app on various browsers and devices to ensure compatibility.

Desktop Deployment

Deploying a Flutter desktop app involves a few different considerations:

1. **Build Your App**: Use flutter build commands to build

your app for the desired desktop platforms: Windows, macOS, or Linux.

2. **Platform-Specific Packaging**: For each platform, you'll need to create platform-specific packages:

– For Windows: Use tools like Inno Setup or WiX Toolset to create an installer for Windows. Package your app as an MSI or EXE file.

– For macOS: Create a DMG file using tools like create-dmg. Follow macOS app distribution guidelines.

– For Linux: Distribute your app as an AppImage, Snap package, or Debian package (.deb).

1. **Code Signing**: Consider code signing your desktop app for security and trustworthiness. Code signing is especially important on macOS and Windows.
2. **Distribution Channels**: Choose distribution channels for your desktop app:

– **Official App Stores**: Consider publishing your app on platforms like Microsoft Store for Windows, Mac App Store for macOS, or Snapcraft for Linux.

– **Website Distribution**: Make your app available for download from your website. Provide clear instructions for installation.

– **Package Managers**: If applicable, distribute your Linux app through package managers like APT or Snapcraft.

1. **Installer and Auto-Update**: Implement an installer for your Windows app, and consider adding auto-update

functionality for a smoother user experience.
2. **Testing**: Thoroughly test your desktop app on each supported platform to ensure it functions correctly.

Cross-Platform Considerations

When deploying for both web and desktop, keep these cross-platform considerations in mind:

- **User Experience**: Ensure that your app provides a consistent and intuitive user experience across all platforms. Test extensively to identify and address any platform-specific issues.

- **Assets**: Verify that all assets (images, fonts, etc.) are correctly packaged and displayed on both web and desktop.

- **Responsive Design**: Confirm that your app's layout adapts to various screen sizes and orientations on both web and desktop.

- **Performance**: Optimize your app's performance to run smoothly on web browsers and desktop systems with varying hardware capabilities.

- **Browser Compatibility**: Test your web app on multiple web browsers, considering different browser-specific behaviors and limitations.

- **Updates**: Plan for regular updates and improvements for both web and desktop versions of your app.

Deploying Flutter apps to web and desktop platforms allows you to reach a broader audience. By following these deployment guidelines and considering the unique characteristics of each platform, you can ensure a successful deployment that provides users with a seamless and reliable experience, whether they access your app through a web browser or install it on their desktop operating system.

Chapter 13: Scalable App Architecture

In Chapter 13, we delve into the critical topic of app architecture for Flutter development. Scalability is a crucial aspect of any app, especially when it comes to larger and more complex projects. In this chapter, we explore various design patterns, structuring strategies, and best practices for building scalable Flutter applications. Let's start by understanding the importance of design patterns in Flutter development.

Section 13.1: Design Patterns for Flutter Development

Design patterns are proven solutions to common software design problems. They provide a structured way of organizing code, enhancing maintainability, and promoting code reusability. In the context of Flutter, using design patterns becomes essential as your application grows in complexity.

The Role of Design Patterns

Design patterns offer several benefits when applied to Flutter development:

1. **Modularity**: Design patterns help break down your app into smaller, manageable parts. This modularity simplifies the development process and allows developers to focus on specific components without worrying about the entire application.
2. **Code Reusability**: Many design patterns encourage code reuse. You can apply the same pattern in different parts of your app, reducing redundant code and improving consistency.

3. **Scalability**: With a well-structured architecture, your app becomes more scalable. You can add new features or make changes without affecting the entire codebase.
4. **Maintenance**: Design patterns make your codebase easier to maintain. When issues arise or updates are needed, you can address them in a structured manner.

Common Design Patterns in Flutter

Flutter developers commonly use the following design patterns:

1. MVC (Model-View-Controller)

- **Model**: Represents the data and business logic of your app.
- **View**: Handles the UI and user interaction.
- **Controller**: Acts as an intermediary, managing data flow between the Model and View.

2. MVVM (Model-View-ViewModel)

- **Model**: Contains the data and business logic.
- **View**: Handles UI rendering.
- **ViewModel**: Manages the presentation logic, serving as a bridge between the Model and View.

3. BLoC (Business Logic Component)

- **Bloc**: Contains the business logic and state management.

- **Events**: Trigger actions and changes in the Bloc.
- **UI Components**: Display the data based on the Bloc's state.

4. Provider

- **ChangeNotifier**: Manages and notifies listeners of changes in data.
- **Consumer**: Listens to changes and rebuilds UI components when data updates.

5. Redux

- **Store**: Holds the app's state.
- **Actions**: Trigger changes to the state.
- **Reducers**: Specify how the state changes based on actions.
- **Middleware**: Handles side effects like asynchronous operations.

Choosing the Right Design Pattern

Selecting the appropriate design pattern depends on your app's requirements, complexity, and your team's familiarity with the pattern. It's common to use a combination of patterns in a Flutter app to address different concerns.

In the upcoming sections, we'll explore how to implement these design patterns in Flutter, providing practical examples and best practices for each. By the end of this chapter, you'll have a deep understanding of how to architect your Flutter app for scalability, maintainability, and code reusability.

Section 13.2: Organizing and Structuring Large Projects

When working on large-scale Flutter projects, maintaining code organization and structure is crucial for readability, collaboration, and maintainability. In this section, we will explore strategies and best practices for organizing and structuring your Flutter codebase effectively.

Folder Structure

A well-defined folder structure helps in keeping your project organized. Consider adopting a structure like the following:

lib/

|—*main.dart*

|—*screens/*

| |—*home_screen.dart*

| |—*profile_screen.dart*

| |—...

|—*widgets/*

| |—*custom_button.dart*

| |—*app_drawer.dart*

| |—...

|—*models/*

| |—*user.dart*

| |—*product.dart*

| |—...

|—*services/*

| |—*api_service.dart*

| |—*database_service.dart*

| |—...

|—*blocs/*

| |—*auth_bloc.dart*

| |—*cart_bloc.dart*

| |—...

|—*utils/*

| |—*helpers.dart*

| |—*constants.dart*

| |—...

|—*routes.dart*

|—*theme.dart*

Breaking down your project into logical folders such as screens, widgets, models, services, blocs, and utils makes it easier to locate and manage specific pieces of functionality.

Modularization

Modularization involves dividing your application into smaller, reusable modules or packages. Each module should have a clear responsibility and interface, making it easier to develop and test.

For instance, if you are building an e-commerce app, you might have separate modules for user authentication, product catalog, shopping cart, and payment processing. This separation allows different teams or developers to work on specific modules independently.

Naming Conventions

Consistent naming conventions help in quickly understanding the purpose of files, classes, and variables. Here are some common conventions in Flutter:

- **File Names**: Use descriptive file names in lowercase with underscores. For example, user_profile_screen.dart is more informative than profile.dart.

- **Class Names**: Follow the UpperCamelCase (PascalCase) convention for class names. For instance, UserProfileScreen.

- **Variable and Function Names**: Use lowerCamelCase for variables and function names. For example, getUserProfileData().

Separation of Concerns

The principle of Separation of Concerns (SoC) suggests that different aspects of your application should be handled separately. In Flutter, this often means separating the UI (presentation) from business logic and data management.

- **UI Components**: Widgets and UI-related code should focus on rendering and user interaction. Minimize business logic within widgets.

- **Business Logic**: Keep business logic separate from widgets. Use BLoCs, Provider, or similar patterns to manage business logic independently.

- **Data Management**: Use services or repositories to handle data fetching, storage, and transformation. This ensures a clear separation of data concerns.

Documentation

Thorough documentation is essential for large projects. Consider adopting documentation tools like DartDoc or generating API documentation to help developers understand your codebase.

Version Control and Collaboration

Utilize version control systems like Git to track changes and collaborate effectively. Establish branching strategies and code review processes to maintain code quality and consistency.

By implementing these strategies, you can effectively organize and structure large Flutter projects, making them more maintainable and scalable as they grow in complexity and size.

Section 13.3: Dependency Injection and Modularization

In large-scale Flutter projects, dependency injection and modularization play a crucial role in maintaining code quality, testability, and reusability. This section will delve into these concepts and their application in Flutter development.

Dependency Injection (DI)

Dependency injection is a design pattern that helps manage dependencies between different parts of your application. In Flutter, the primary way to implement DI is by using packages like provider and get_it. Here's how it works:

1. **Register Dependencies**: Create instances of classes or services you want to use throughout your app and register them using a DI container. For example, you can register an API service or a database helper.
2. **Inject Dependencies**: Inject these registered dependencies into classes or widgets that need them. This is typically done through constructor injection or method injection.

```
class UserProfileScreen extends StatelessWidget {

final ApiService apiService;

UserProfileScreen({required this.apiService});

@override

Widget build(BuildContext context) {

// Use apiService to fetch user data.

}

}
```

By injecting dependencies, you can easily swap implementations, mock services for testing, and ensure loose coupling between components.

Modularization

Modularization involves breaking down your application into smaller, self-contained modules or packages. Each module can have its own set of screens, widgets, business logic, and dependencies. Modularization provides several benefits:

1. **Reusability**: Modules can be reused across different projects or within the same project, promoting code efficiency.
2. **Scalability**: As your app grows, you can add new modules without affecting existing ones, making it easier to manage complexity.
3. **Team Collaboration**: Different teams or developers can work on separate modules independently, speeding up development.
4. **Testing**: Modules can be tested in isolation, ensuring that they work correctly before integration.

For example, in a large e-commerce app, you might have separate modules for authentication, product catalog, shopping cart, and payment processing. Each module can encapsulate its own logic and dependencies.

Using Provider for Dependency Injection

The provider package in Flutter is a popular choice for implementing DI. It offers various provider types, such as Provider, ChangeNotifierProvider, and StreamProvider, which facilitate the injection of dependencies into widgets.

Here's a simplified example of using provider for DI:

```
void main() {
runApp(
MultiProvider(
providers: [
Provider<ApiService>(
create: (_) => ApiService(),
),
Provider<DatabaseService>(
create: (_) => DatabaseService(),
),
],
child: MyApp(),
),
);
}
```

In the code above, we use Provider to register ApiService and DatabaseService. These services can now be injected into widgets anywhere in the widget tree.

Modularization with Flutter Packages

To achieve modularization in Flutter, consider creating separate packages for different modules or features of your app. Each package can have its own folder structure, dependencies, and entry points. You can then import and use these packages in your main app.

For example, you might have a separate Flutter package for user authentication that includes screens, services, and widgets related to authentication. This package can be developed and tested independently before integrating it into your main app.

By combining dependency injection and modularization, you can create scalable, maintainable, and testable Flutter apps, even as they grow in complexity and size. These practices contribute to code organization and help streamline development processes.

Section 13.4: Scalable Data Management Strategies

In Flutter applications, effective data management is crucial, especially in large-scale projects. This section explores strategies for managing and handling data to ensure scalability, maintainability, and optimal performance.

State Management

State management is a fundamental aspect of Flutter app development, and choosing the right approach is essential. Different state management solutions cater to various project sizes and complexity levels:

1. **Provider and Riverpod**: These packages offer a simple and scalable solution for managing state, especially in small to

medium-sized projects. They follow the provider pattern, which enables the injection of dependencies and state into your widgets.

```
final counterProvider = Provider<int>((ref) => 0);

class CounterWidget extends ConsumerWidget {

@override

Widget build(BuildContext context, ScopedReader watch) {

final count = watch(counterProvider);

return Text('Count: $count');

}

}
```

1. **Bloc Pattern**: The Bloc pattern is a popular choice for managing complex state in Flutter apps. It's suitable for medium to large-scale projects. The flutter_bloc package simplifies implementing this pattern.

```
class CounterCubit extends Cubit<int> {

CounterCubit() : super(0);

void increment() => emit(state + 1);

}

final counterCubit = CounterCubit();

class CounterWidget extends StatelessWidget {
```

```
@override
Widget build(BuildContext context) {
return BlocBuilder<CounterCubit, int>(
builder: (context, state) {
return Text('Count: $state');
},
);
}
}
```

1. **Redux**: Redux is another state management approach that works well in large-scale projects. The redux package provides the necessary tools to implement this pattern.

```
// Define actions and reducers
final store = Store<int>(
counterReducer,
initialState: 0,
);
class CounterWidget extends StatelessWidget {
@override
Widget build(BuildContext context) {
```

```
return StoreConnector<int, int>(

converter: (store) => store.state,

builder: (context, count) {

return Text('Count: $count');

},

);

}

}
```

Caching and Data Fetching

Efficient data caching and fetching mechanisms are crucial for optimizing app performance, especially when dealing with large datasets or remote APIs:

1. **Offline Data Storage**: Utilize local storage solutions like SQLite databases (using packages like sqflite) or key-value stores (using shared_preferences) for caching frequently used data, minimizing the need for network requests.
2. **Data Pagination**: Implement pagination techniques when dealing with large lists of data. Load data in chunks or pages to reduce the initial load time and provide a smoother user experience.
3. **Data Prefetching**: Implement data prefetching strategies to load data in the background, anticipating user actions. This can be useful in applications with heavy data requirements.

API Requests and Rate Limiting

Managing API requests efficiently is essential for large-scale Flutter apps that interact with external services:

1. **Rate Limiting**: When interacting with external APIs, be mindful of rate limiting imposed by the service providers. Implement strategies like exponential backoff and rate limiting queues to handle API requests gracefully and prevent overloading.
2. **Caching API Responses**: Cache API responses locally to reduce the number of duplicate requests. This can help improve app responsiveness and reduce the load on the server.
3. **Network Connectivity Handling**: Implement robust network connectivity handling to gracefully manage scenarios where the device may be offline or have limited connectivity.

Data Security and Encryption

In large-scale apps, data security is of utmost importance. Consider these practices:

1. **Data Encryption**: Implement encryption for sensitive data stored locally or transmitted over the network. Use packages like encrypt for secure data handling.
2. **Authentication and Authorization**: Ensure proper authentication and authorization mechanisms are in place to protect data from unauthorized access.
3. **Data Validation**: Validate incoming data from external sources to prevent security vulnerabilities like SQL injection or cross-site scripting (XSS).

By applying these scalable data management strategies, you can build Flutter apps that are efficient, maintainable, and capable of handling complex data requirements in large-scale scenarios.

Section 13.5: Ensuring Quality with Code Reviews and Documentation

In large-scale Flutter projects, maintaining code quality is paramount to ensure the longevity and stability of the application. This section discusses the importance of code reviews and documentation in the development process.

Code Reviews

Code reviews are a critical part of any software development workflow, and they become even more essential in large-scale projects. Here are some key practices for effective code reviews:

1. **Peer Review Process**: Establish a formal code review process where team members review each other's code before it gets merged into the main codebase. Use tools like GitHub Pull Requests or GitLab Merge Requests to facilitate the process.
2. **Coding Standards**: Define and enforce coding standards and style guides for your Flutter project. This ensures consistency and readability across the codebase.
3. **Checklist for Reviews**: Create a checklist of common issues to look for during code reviews. This might include code formatting, error handling, and adherence to best practices.
4. **Automated Code Analysis**: Use static analysis tools like dart analyze or linters (e.g., pedantic) to catch common issues automatically. Integrate these tools into your CI/CD

pipeline.

5. **Code Review Comments**: Provide constructive feedback during code reviews. Focus on clarity, maintainability, and potential performance bottlenecks. Encourage discussions and knowledge sharing.
6. **Regular Review Meetings**: For large-scale projects, consider holding regular code review meetings where team members can discuss complex changes or architectural decisions.

Documentation

Comprehensive documentation is vital for large-scale Flutter projects to onboard new team members, maintain codebases, and understand project architecture. Here are key aspects of effective documentation:

1. **Code Comments**: Include inline comments explaining non-trivial sections of code. Comments should clarify the intent, logic, and any dependencies. However, strive for self-documenting code when possible.

// Good Comment Example

final result = calculateTotal(items); // Calculate total cost.

// Bad Comment Example (redundant)

final result = calculateTotal(items); // Calculate the total cost of items.

1. **API Documentation**: Document public APIs, classes, and methods. Use tools like dartdoc to generate API

documentation from code comments. Ensure that the generated documentation is accessible to the team.

2. **Project Wiki**: Create a project wiki or README.md file that provides an overview of the project, its architecture, and how to set up a development environment. Include installation instructions and any prerequisites.
3. **Codebase Structure**: Document the high-level structure of your Flutter app, including the organization of directories, modules, and packages. Explain the purpose of each major component.
4. **Coding Guidelines**: Include a section in your documentation that outlines coding guidelines, best practices, and coding standards followed by your team. This helps ensure consistency in code style.
5. **Change Logs**: Maintain a changelog or release notes document that tracks significant changes, bug fixes, and enhancements in each version of your application.
6. **Troubleshooting Guides**: Create troubleshooting guides for common issues that developers may encounter during development or when using the application.
7. **User Documentation**: If your Flutter app is customer-facing, create user documentation or help guides to assist end-users in using the application effectively.

Remember that documentation is an ongoing effort. It should evolve alongside your project, reflecting changes in codebase, architecture, and best practices. Encourage team members to contribute to and update documentation regularly.

By prioritizing code reviews and maintaining comprehensive documentation, you can ensure that your large-scale Flutter project remains manageable, maintainable, and accessible to your development team, regardless of its size or complexity.

Chapter 14: Real-Time Applications and Streaming

Real-time applications have become increasingly popular in the digital landscape. These applications provide users with live, up-to-date information and enable instant communication. Flutter, with its robust ecosystem of packages and plugins, allows developers to create real-time applications and implement features like chat systems, live data updates, and streaming content.

In this chapter, we will explore various aspects of building real-time applications and implementing streaming features in Flutter. We will cover topics such as WebSockets for real-time data, creating chat applications, streaming video and audio, and optimizing real-time data handling. Additionally, we will examine real-world case studies of Flutter apps that leverage real-time features.

Section 14.1: Implementing Real-Time Data with WebSockets

WebSockets are a communication protocol that enables bidirectional, real-time data transfer between a client and a server. They are commonly used for building real-time features in web and mobile applications, including chat systems, live notifications, and collaborative tools.

Why WebSockets?

WebSockets offer several advantages for real-time communication:

- **Low Latency**: WebSockets maintain a persistent connection, allowing data to be transmitted with minimal delay, making them suitable for real-time scenarios.

- **Bi-Directional**: WebSockets enable data to flow in both directions, from the server to the client and vice versa, facilitating interactive and responsive applications.

- **Efficient**: Unlike traditional HTTP requests, which require the client to poll the server for updates, WebSockets eliminate the need for constant polling, reducing unnecessary network traffic.

Implementing WebSockets in Flutter

To implement WebSockets in your Flutter application, you can use packages like web_socket_channel and socket_io_client. Here's a basic example of setting up a WebSocket connection:

```
import 'package:flutter/material.dart';

import 'package:web_socket_channel/web_socket_channel.dart';

import 'package:web_socket_channel/io.dart'; // Use 'io' for Flutter web, 'io' for Flutter mobile

void main() => runApp(MyApp());

class MyApp extends StatelessWidget {

final WebSocketChannel channel = IOWebSocketChannel.connect('wss://example.com/ws');

@override

Widget build(BuildContext context) {

return MaterialApp(

title: 'WebSocket Demo',
```

```
home: Scaffold(
appBar: AppBar(
title: Text('WebSocket Demo'),
),
body: StreamBuilder(
stream: channel.stream,
builder: (context, snapshot) {
return Center(
child: Text(snapshot.hasData ? 'Received: ${snapshot.data}' : 'No Data'),
);
},
),
floatingActionButton: FloatingActionButton(
onPressed: () {
channel.sink.add('Hello, WebSocket!');
},
child: Icon(Icons.send),
),
),
);
```

```
}
@override
void dispose() {
channel.sink.close();
super.dispose();
}
}
```

In this example, we establish a WebSocket connection to a server, listen for incoming data, and send data to the server when the user presses a button. The web_socket_channel package simplifies WebSocket integration in Flutter, making it easier to incorporate real-time features into your applications.

WebSockets are a powerful tool for building real-time Flutter applications, enabling developers to create responsive and interactive user experiences. In the following sections of this chapter, we will explore more real-time application scenarios and their implementation in Flutter.

Section 14.2: Building Chat Applications

Chat applications have become an integral part of modern communication, offering real-time messaging between users. Flutter provides a robust framework for building chat applications that can be used for personal chats, group conversations, customer support, and more. In this section, we will explore the key components and considerations for building chat applications in Flutter.

Key Features of Chat Applications

Successful chat applications typically include the following key features:

1. **Real-Time Messaging**: Users can send and receive messages instantly, creating a seamless conversation experience.
2. **User Authentication**: Secure user authentication ensures that only authorized users can access the chat.
3. **Message Persistence**: Chat history should be stored and synchronized across devices, allowing users to access their messages from multiple platforms.
4. **Notifications**: Users receive notifications for new messages, even when the app is in the background.
5. **User Profiles**: Users can create profiles, set profile pictures, and manage their information.

Implementing Chat Features

To build a chat application in Flutter, you can follow these general steps:

1. **User Authentication**: Implement user authentication using Firebase Authentication, OAuth, or any other authentication service of your choice.
2. **Database Integration**: Use a database to store and retrieve chat messages. Firebase Realtime Database or Firestore are popular choices for real-time chat applications.
3. **Real-Time Messaging**: Implement real-time messaging using WebSockets or Firebase Cloud Messaging (FCM) for push notifications.
4. **UI Design**: Create an intuitive and user-friendly chat UI with Flutter widgets. You can use packages like

chat_bubble for message bubbles and emoji_picker for emojis.

5. **Message Persistence**: Store chat history in the database and synchronize it across devices using Firebase or other synchronization techniques.
6. **Notifications**: Set up push notifications to notify users of new messages, even when the app is in the background.
7. **User Profiles**: Allow users to create profiles and set profile pictures. You can use Firebase Authentication for user profiles.

Example Chat App Code

Here's a simplified example of a chat application UI in Flutter:

```
import 'package:flutter/material.dart';

void main() {

runApp(ChatApp());

}

class ChatApp extends StatelessWidget {

@override

Widget build(BuildContext context) {

return MaterialApp(

title: 'Chat App',

home: ChatScreen(),

);
```

```
}
}
class ChatScreen extends StatefulWidget {
@override
State createState() => ChatScreenState();
}
class ChatScreenState extends State<ChatScreen> {
final TextEditingController _textController = TextEditingController();
final List<ChatMessage> _messages = <ChatMessage>[];
void _handleSubmitted(String text) {
_textController.clear();
ChatMessage message = ChatMessage(
text: text,
);
setState(() {
_messages.insert(0, message);
});
}
@override
Widget build(BuildContext context) {
```

```
return Scaffold(
appBar: AppBar(
title: Text('Chat App'),
),
body: Column(
children: <Widget>[
Flexible(
child: ListView.builder(
padding: EdgeInsets.all(8.0),
reverse: true,
itemBuilder: (_, int index) => _messages[index],
itemCount: _messages.length,
),
),
Divider(height: 1.0),
Container(
decoration: BoxDecoration(
color: Theme.of(context).cardColor,
),
child: _buildTextComposer(),
```

```
),
],
),
);
}
Widget _buildTextComposer() {
return IconTheme(
data: IconThemeData(color: Theme.of(context).accentColor),
child: Container(
margin: EdgeInsets.symmetric(horizontal: 8.0),
child: Row(
children: <Widget>[
Flexible(
child: TextField(
controller: _textController,
onSubmitted: _handleSubmitted,
decoration: InputDecoration.collapsed(hintText: 'Send a message'),
),
),
IconButton(
```

```
icon: Icon(Icons.send),
onPressed: () => _handleSubmitted(_textController.text),
),
],
),
),
);
}
}
class ChatMessage extends StatelessWidget {
ChatMessage({required this.text});
final String text;
@override
Widget build(BuildContext context) {
return Container(
margin: EdgeInsets.symmetric(vertical: 10.0),
child: Text(text),
);
}
}
```

This code provides a basic chat interface where users can send and receive messages. To create a fully functional chat application, you would need to integrate authentication, database storage, real-time messaging, and push notifications, as mentioned earlier.

Building a chat application in Flutter is an exciting project that allows you to explore real-time communication and user interface design. Depending on your requirements, you can enhance this example with more features and integrations to create a robust chat experience.

Section 14.3: Streaming Video and Audio

Streaming video and audio has become an integral part of modern applications, offering users access to live content and media playback. In this section, we'll explore how to integrate streaming video and audio features into your Flutter applications.

Key Considerations for Streaming

Before implementing streaming in your Flutter app, it's important to consider the following aspects:

1. **Content Source**: Determine the source of your streaming content. It could be a live video feed, recorded videos, audio podcasts, or any other form of media.
2. **Streaming Protocol**: Choose the appropriate streaming protocol, such as HTTP Live Streaming (HLS), Dynamic Adaptive Streaming over HTTP (DASH), or Real-Time Messaging Protocol (RTMP), based on your content source and requirements.
3. **Media Player**: Select a media player library or plugin for Flutter. Popular choices include the video_player and

audioplayers plugins, which provide native-like media playback experiences.

4. **User Experience**: Design a user-friendly interface for controlling media playback, including play, pause, seek, and volume controls.
5. **Streaming Backend**: Set up a server or backend infrastructure capable of serving streaming content. This may involve using services like Amazon S3, CloudFront, or third-party streaming providers.

Integrating Video Streaming

To integrate video streaming in your Flutter app, you can use the video_player package. Here's a simplified example of how to use it:

```
import 'package:flutter/material.dart';

import 'package:video_player/video_player.dart';

void main() {

runApp(VideoPlayerApp());

}

class VideoPlayerApp extends StatelessWidget {

@override

Widget build(BuildContext context) {

return MaterialApp(

home: Scaffold(

appBar: AppBar(
```

```
title: Text('Video Player Example'),
),
body: Center(
child: VideoPlayerScreen(),
),
),
);
}
}
class VideoPlayerScreen extends StatefulWidget {
@override
_VideoPlayerScreenState createState() =>
_VideoPlayerScreenState();
}
class _VideoPlayerScreenState extends State<VideoPlayerScreen> {
late VideoPlayerController _controller;
@override
void initState() {
super.initState();
_controller = VideoPlayerController.network(
'https://example.com/sample.mp4',
```

```
)
..initialize().then((_) {
// Ensure the first frame is shown and the video is ready to play.
setState(() {});
});
}
@override
Widget build(BuildContext context) {
return Center(
child: _controller.value.isInitialized
? AspectRatio(
aspectRatio: _controller.value.aspectRatio,
child: VideoPlayer(_controller),
)
: CircularProgressIndicator(), // Show a loading indicator until video is initialized.
);
}
@override
void dispose() {
super.dispose();
```

```
_controller.dispose();
}
}
```

This code creates a simple Flutter app that plays a video from a network source. You can customize it to suit your streaming content source and design preferences.

Integrating Audio Streaming

For audio streaming, the audioplayers package is commonly used. Here's a basic example of how to integrate audio streaming:

```
import 'package:flutter/material.dart';
import 'package:audioplayers/audioplayers.dart';
void main() {
runApp(AudioPlayerApp());
}
class AudioPlayerApp extends StatelessWidget {
@override
Widget build(BuildContext context) {
return MaterialApp(
home: Scaffold(
appBar: AppBar(
title: Text('Audio Player Example'),
```

```
),
body: Center(
child: AudioPlayerScreen(),
),
),
);
}
}
class AudioPlayerScreen extends StatefulWidget {
@override
_AudioPlayerScreenState createState() =>
_AudioPlayerScreenState();
}
class _AudioPlayerScreenState extends State<AudioPlayerScreen> {
late AudioPlayer audioPlayer;
String audioUrl = 'https://example.com/audio.mp3';
@override
void initState() {
super.initState();
audioPlayer = AudioPlayer();
audioPlayer.setUrl(audioUrl);
```

```
}
@override
Widget build(BuildContext context) {
return Column(
mainAxisAlignment: MainAxisAlignment.center,
crossAxisAlignment: CrossAxisAlignment.center,
children: [
IconButton(
icon: Icon(Icons.play_arrow),
onPressed: () => audioPlayer.play(audioUrl),
),
IconButton(
icon: Icon(Icons.pause),
onPressed: () => audioPlayer.pause(),
),
IconButton(
icon: Icon(Icons.stop),
onPressed: () => audioPlayer.stop(),
),
],
```

```
);
}
@override
void dispose() {
super.dispose();
audioPlayer.dispose();
}
}
```

This code sets up an audio player that can play audio from a specified URL. You can extend it to add more features like seeking, volume control, and displaying audio playback progress.

Integrating streaming video and audio into your Flutter app opens up possibilities for delivering engaging multimedia content to your users. Depending on your project's requirements, you can enhance these examples with additional features and customize the player's appearance and behavior to match your app's design.

Section 14.4: Handling Real-Time Data Efficiently

Handling real-time data efficiently is crucial for building responsive and interactive Flutter applications. This section explores techniques and best practices for managing real-time data updates, ensuring that your app remains synchronized with changing data sources.

The Importance of Real-Time Data

Many modern applications, such as social media platforms, messaging apps, and collaborative tools, rely on real-time data to provide users with up-to-the-minute information. Real-time data updates enhance user engagement and improve the overall user experience.

WebSocket for Real-Time Communication

WebSocket is a communication protocol that enables bidirectional, full-duplex communication channels over a single TCP connection. It's widely used for implementing real-time features in web and mobile applications. In Flutter, you can use packages like web_socket_channel to work with WebSockets.

Here's a simplified example of how to set up a WebSocket connection in Flutter:

```
import 'package:flutter/material.dart';

import 'package:web_socket_channel/web_socket_channel.dart';

void main() => runApp(MyApp());

class MyApp extends StatelessWidget {

final WebSocketChannel channel = WebSocketChannel.connect(

Uri.parse('wss://example.com/ws'),

);

@override

Widget build(BuildContext context) {
```

```
return MaterialApp(
home: Scaffold(
appBar: AppBar(
title: Text('WebSocket Example'),
),
body: Center(
child: StreamBuilder(
stream: channel.stream,
builder: (context, snapshot) {
if (snapshot.hasError) {
return Text('Error: ${snapshot.error}');
}
if (snapshot.hasData) {
return Text('Received: ${snapshot.data}');
}
return CircularProgressIndicator();
},
),
),
),
```

```
);
}
}
```

This code establishes a WebSocket connection and displays data received from the server. It's a basic example that you can expand upon to implement real-time features in your app.

Firebase Realtime Database

Firebase, a popular backend service provided by Google, offers the Firebase Realtime Database, which is well-suited for real-time data synchronization. It provides a cloud-hosted NoSQL database that can be easily integrated into Flutter apps.

To get started with Firebase Realtime Database in Flutter, follow these steps:

1. Create a Firebase project in the Firebase Console (https://console.firebase.google.com/).
2. Add your Flutter app to the project and download the Firebase configuration file.
3. Add the Firebase packages to your pubspec.yaml file.

Here's an example of how to use Firebase Realtime Database in Flutter:

```
import 'package:flutter/material.dart';

import 'package:firebase_core/firebase_core.dart';

import 'package:firebase_database/firebase_database.dart';

void main() async {
```

```
WidgetsFlutterBinding.ensureInitialized();
await Firebase.initializeApp();
runApp(MyApp());
}
class MyApp extends StatelessWidget {
final DatabaseReference _database = FirebaseDatabase.instance.reference();
@override
Widget build(BuildContext context) {
return MaterialApp(
home: Scaffold(
appBar: AppBar(
title: Text('Firebase Realtime Database Example'),
),
body: Center(
child: StreamBuilder(
stream: _database.child('messages').onValue,
builder: (context, snapshot) {
if (snapshot.hasError) {
return Text('Error: ${snapshot.error}');
}
```

```
if (snapshot.hasData) {
final data = snapshot.data.snapshot.value;
return Text('Data from Firebase: $data');
}
return CircularProgressIndicator();
},
),
),
),
);
}
}
```

In this example, the app reads and displays data from the Firebase Realtime Database. You can adapt this code to write data to the database and respond to real-time updates.

Optimizing Real-Time Data Management

Efficiently managing real-time data involves minimizing unnecessary updates and optimizing network usage. Consider the following best practices:

1. Use WebSocket or Firebase for real-time communication, as they are optimized for such use cases.
2. Implement data caching and synchronization strategies to minimize the impact of network latency.

3. Avoid frequent polling of data and use push notifications or server-sent events when applicable.
4. Apply throttling and debouncing techniques to control the rate of data updates and user interface changes.
5. Optimize data structures and queries to reduce the amount of data transmitted and processed.

By following these best practices and leveraging appropriate tools and libraries, you can build Flutter apps that provide a seamless and responsive real-time experience for your users. Real-time data features can be a significant asset for various applications, ranging from chat apps to collaborative tools and live event tracking.

Section 14.5: Case Studies of Real-Time Flutter Apps

In this section, we'll explore several case studies of real-world Flutter applications that effectively utilize real-time features to enhance user experiences. These case studies showcase how Flutter can be employed to build real-time applications across different domains.

1. Chat Application

One of the most common use cases for real-time Flutter apps is chat applications. Whether it's a one-on-one chat or a group chat, Flutter provides the tools and libraries to create a real-time chat experience. Firebase Realtime Database or Firestore can be used as the backend to store and sync messages in real-time. Additionally, packages like cloud_firestore and firebase_auth make it easy to implement features like user authentication and real-time messaging.

2. Live Sports Scores

Sports apps often require real-time updates for scores, game events, and news. Flutter can be used to create sports apps that provide live updates for various sports, such as football, basketball, or cricket. APIs like WebSocket can deliver real-time score updates to the app, ensuring users stay informed about their favorite teams and matches.

3. Collaborative Task Management

Task management and project collaboration tools benefit greatly from real-time features. Flutter can be used to build applications where multiple users can collaborate on tasks, projects, or to-do lists in real-time. Firebase Realtime Database or other real-time databases enable synchronized task updates and instant notifications when changes occur.

4. Live Auctions and Bidding

Real-time Flutter apps can also be applied in the e-commerce domain, particularly for live auctions and bidding platforms. Users can place bids in real-time, and the app can display live updates of current bids and auction progress. WebSocket or Firebase can handle real-time communication between users and the server, ensuring a seamless bidding experience.

5. Location Sharing and Tracking

Apps that involve location sharing or tracking, such as ride-sharing and delivery services, require real-time location updates. Flutter can be used to create apps that provide real-time tracking of drivers or deliveries on a map. Services like Firebase Realtime Database can store and transmit location data in real-time, allowing users to track their orders or rides.

6. Live Streaming and Video Conferencing

Live streaming apps and video conferencing tools rely heavily on real-time communication. Flutter, combined with platforms like Agora or WebRTC, can be used to develop applications that support live streaming, video calls, and webinars. These apps enable real-time interactions between hosts and participants, making them suitable for various domains, including education, entertainment, and business.

7. Real-Time Collaboration Tools

Collaboration tools for remote teams can leverage real-time Flutter features to enhance productivity. Applications can include features like real-time document editing, instant messaging, and collaborative whiteboards. WebSocket or Firebase can facilitate real-time data synchronization among team members, allowing them to work together seamlessly, regardless of their locations.

8. Social Media Feeds

Social media apps, such as Twitter or Instagram clones, require real-time updates of user feeds, comments, and notifications. Flutter can be used to create such apps, and Firebase can handle real-time data storage and synchronization. Users can receive instant notifications when someone likes their posts or comments on their content.

These case studies demonstrate the versatility of Flutter in building real-time applications across various domains. By utilizing the appropriate tools, libraries, and backend services, developers can create responsive and engaging Flutter apps that keep users connected and informed in real-time. Whether it's enhancing user communication, delivering live updates, or enabling collaborative work, Flutter's capabilities make it a powerful choice for real-time app development.

Chapter 15: Working with Sensors and Hardware

Section 15.1: Accessing Device Sensors

In this section, we'll explore how Flutter allows developers to access and utilize various device sensors, enabling the creation of sensor-driven applications that can gather data from a device's hardware components. Device sensors include a wide range of hardware components, such as accelerometers, gyroscopes, GPS receivers, magnetometers, light sensors, proximity sensors, and more. Flutter provides plugins and libraries to interact with these sensors, making it possible to build applications that respond to real-world physical data.

Flutter Sensor Plugins

Flutter offers a collection of plugins and packages that simplify the process of working with sensors. Some of the commonly used sensor plugins include:

1. **Sensors Package**: The sensors package is an official Flutter package that provides access to various hardware sensors, such as the accelerometer, gyroscope, magnetometer, and more. Developers can use this package to listen to sensor data and integrate it into their applications.

```
import 'package:sensors/sensors.dart';

accelerometerEvents.listen((AccelerometerEvent event) {

// Handle accelerometer data
```

```
double x = event.x;

double y = event.y;

double z = event.z;

});
```

1. **Location Package**: For GPS-related tasks, the location package is commonly used. It allows Flutter apps to access the device's GPS location data, making it possible to create location-based applications, such as mapping and navigation apps.

```
import 'package:location/location.dart';

Location location = Location();

LocationData locationData = await location.getLocation();

double latitude = locationData.latitude;

double longitude = locationData.longitude;
```

1. **FlutterBlue**: FlutterBlue is a popular package for working with Bluetooth Low Energy (BLE) devices. It enables Flutter apps to communicate with and control Bluetooth peripherals, making it suitable for applications involving IoT (Internet of Things) devices or custom sensor hardware.

```
import 'package:flutter_blue/flutter_blue.dart';

FlutterBlue flutterBlue = FlutterBlue.instance;
```

```
// Scan for nearby BLE devices

flutterBlue.scan().listen((ScanResult result) {

// Handle discovered BLE devices

});
```

1. **Barcode Scanner**: Barcode scanning is another sensor-related task that can be accomplished with Flutter using plugins like barcode_scan. These plugins allow Flutter apps to use the device's camera to scan barcodes and QR codes.

```
import 'package:barcode_scan/barcode_scan.dart';

String barcode = await BarcodeScanner.scan();
```

Use Cases for Sensor-Driven Apps

The ability to access device sensors opens up a wide range of use cases for Flutter applications. Here are some examples:

- **Fitness and Health Apps**: Flutter apps can use accelerometer and GPS data to track users' physical activities, such as steps taken, distance traveled, and location-based statistics. These apps are popular for fitness and health monitoring.

- **Augmented Reality (AR) Apps**: AR applications often rely on device sensors like accelerometers and gyroscopes to create interactive and immersive experiences. Flutter can be used to build AR apps that respond to users' movements.

- **Navigation and Maps**: Location-based apps, such as maps and navigation tools, make extensive use of GPS and sensor data to provide users with real-time directions and location information.

- **IoT Control**: Flutter can be used to build control interfaces for IoT devices. For example, a Flutter app can interact with BLE-enabled sensors and actuators to control smart home appliances.

- **Barcode Scanners**: Inventory management and retail applications often use barcode scanning to track products and manage inventory. Flutter apps can integrate barcode scanning features.

In conclusion, Flutter's support for accessing device sensors and hardware components through various plugins and packages empowers developers to create sensor-driven applications across diverse domains. Whether it's leveraging GPS data for location-based services or utilizing accelerometer readings for motion-based interactions, Flutter provides the tools needed to build innovative and responsive apps that interact with the physical world.

Section 15.2: Bluetooth and NFC Integration

In this section, we'll delve into how Flutter can be used to integrate with Bluetooth and Near Field Communication (NFC) technologies, enabling developers to build applications that communicate with external devices and transfer data wirelessly. Both Bluetooth and NFC have a wide range of applications, from IoT (Internet of Things) control to contactless payments and data sharing.

Bluetooth Integration

Flutter provides a powerful package called flutter_blue that facilitates communication with Bluetooth devices, particularly Bluetooth Low Energy (BLE) peripherals. This package streamlines the process of scanning for nearby BLE devices, connecting to them, and exchanging data.

Here's a high-level overview of integrating Bluetooth in a Flutter app:

1. **Install the Package**: Start by adding the flutter_blue package to your Flutter project's pubspec.yaml file and run flutter pub get to fetch the package.

```
dependencies:

flutter:

sdk: flutter

flutter_blue: ^latest_version
```

1. **Scanning for Devices**: Use the FlutterBlue instance to scan for nearby BLE devices. You can filter devices by specific service UUIDs or other criteria.

```
import 'package:flutter_blue/flutter_blue.dart';

FlutterBlue flutterBlue = FlutterBlue.instance;

// Scan for nearby BLE devices

flutterBlue.scan().listen((ScanResult result) {

// Handle discovered BLE devices
```

```
});
```

1. **Connecting and Communicating**: After discovering a device, you can establish a connection and exchange data with it. Services and characteristics exposed by the peripheral can be accessed and utilized.

```
// Connect to a BLE device

await result.device.connect();

// Discover services

List<BluetoothService> services = await result.device.discoverServices();

// Interact with characteristics

BluetoothCharacteristic characteristic = services.firstWhere(

(service) => service.uuid.toString() == 'your_characteristic_uuid',

).characteristics.first;

// Read data from the characteristic

List<int> data = await characteristic.read();
```

1. **Handling Device Disconnections**: It's important to implement error handling and connection management, as Bluetooth devices can disconnect unexpectedly. You can use FlutterBlue's stream to listen for device connection changes and handle disconnections gracefully.

NFC Integration

Near Field Communication (NFC) allows for short-range wireless communication between devices, making it ideal for contactless data exchange. Flutter offers the flutter_nfc_reader package, which simplifies NFC integration in Flutter apps.

Here's a basic guide to integrating NFC in a Flutter app:

1. **Install the Package**: Add the flutter_nfc_reader package to your pubspec.yaml file and run flutter pub get.

```
dependencies:

flutter:

sdk: flutter

flutter_nfc_reader: ^latest_version
```

1. **Request NFC Permissions**: You'll need to request NFC permissions in your app's AndroidManifest.xml and Info.plist files for Android and iOS, respectively.
2. **Reading NFC Data**: To read NFC data, you can use the NfcData class provided by the package. It allows you to start listening for NFC data and retrieve the scanned NFC tag's information.

```
import 'package:flutter_nfc_reader/flutter_nfc_reader.dart';

// Start listening for NFC data

NFC.isNFCSupported.then((supported) {

if (supported) {
```

```
NFC.read().listen((NfcData data) {
// Handle NFC tag data
String id = data.id;
List<int> content = data.content;
});
}
});
```

1. **Error Handling**: NFC communication may not always be successful, so it's essential to implement error handling to deal with unexpected scenarios gracefully.

Use Cases

Bluetooth and NFC integration in Flutter opens up various use cases:

- **IoT Control**: Flutter apps can connect to and control IoT devices over Bluetooth, allowing users to interact with smart appliances and gadgets from their smartphones.
- **Health and Fitness Devices**: Bluetooth integration is commonly used in health and fitness apps to connect with wearable devices like fitness trackers and heart rate monitors.
- **Contactless Payments**: NFC enables contactless payment solutions. Apps can use NFC to facilitate transactions, making mobile payments quick and convenient.

• **Inventory Management**: NFC can be employed in inventory management apps for scanning NFC tags on products and tracking stock levels.

• **Access Control**: NFC can be used for secure access control systems, allowing users to use their smartphones as keys or access cards.

In summary, Flutter provides the means to integrate with Bluetooth and NFC technologies, offering developers the tools needed to create applications that interact with a wide range of external devices and enable contactless data exchange. Whether you're building IoT control interfaces, health and fitness apps, or contactless payment solutions, Flutter's support for Bluetooth and NFC integration empowers you to bring these features to your mobile applications.

Section 15.3: Using GPS and Location Services

In this section, we'll explore how to harness the power of GPS (Global Positioning System) and location services within Flutter applications. Location-based features are crucial for various types of apps, from navigation and mapping applications to location-aware social networking and local business services. Flutter provides the geolocator package to simplify GPS and location-related tasks.

Installing the geolocator Package

To get started with GPS and location services in Flutter, you can add the geolocator package to your project. Open your pubspec.yaml file and add the package dependency:

dependencies:

```
flutter:

sdk: flutter

geolocator: ^latest_version
```

Then, run flutter pub get to fetch the package.

Requesting Location Permissions

Before accessing a user's location, you need to request location permissions. For Android and iOS, you'll need to configure permissions in the AndroidManifest.xml and Info.plist files, respectively. Additionally, you can request permissions at runtime using the permission_handler package.

Obtaining the User's Location

The geolocator package provides a straightforward way to retrieve the user's current location. Here's a basic example of how to do it:

```
import 'package:flutter/material.dart';

import 'package:geolocator/geolocator.dart';

class LocationScreen extends StatefulWidget {

@override

_LocationScreenState createState() => _LocationScreenState();

}

class _LocationScreenState extends State<LocationScreen> {

Position _currentPosition;

@override
```

```
void initState() {
super.initState();
_getCurrentLocation();
}
void _getCurrentLocation() async {
try {
Position position = await Geolocator.getCurrentPosition(
desiredAccuracy: LocationAccuracy.best,
);
setState(() {
_currentPosition = position;
});
} catch (e) {
print("Error: $e");
}
}
@override
Widget build(BuildContext context) {
return Scaffold(
appBar: AppBar(
```

```
title: Text('User Location'),
),
body: Center(
child: _currentPosition == null
? CircularProgressIndicator()
: Text(
'Latitude: ${_currentPosition.latitude}, Longitude: ${_currentPosition.longitude}',
),
),
);
}
}
```

In the code above, we create a simple Flutter screen that displays the user's current latitude and longitude. The getCurrentPosition method from the geolocator package is used to fetch the location data.

Handling Location Updates

In many cases, you might need to track the user's location continuously. You can achieve this by using the getPositionStream method, which provides a stream of location updates:

```
StreamSubscription<Position> _positionStreamSubscription;
```

```
void _startLocationUpdates() {
_positionStreamSubscription = Geolocator.getPositionStream(
desiredAccuracy: LocationAccuracy.best,
distanceFilter: 10, // Minimum distance (in meters) between updates
).listen((Position position) {
setState(() {
_currentPosition = position;
});
});
}
void _stopLocationUpdates() {
if (_positionStreamSubscription != null) {
_positionStreamSubscription.cancel();
}
}
```

In the code above, we start listening to location updates when _startLocationUpdates is called and stop updates with _stopLocationUpdates. The location data is then updated in the UI.

Geocoding and Reverse Geocoding

The geolocator package also provides geocoding and reverse geocoding capabilities, allowing you to convert between coordinates and human-readable addresses and vice versa.

Here's an example of how to perform reverse geocoding to get an address from coordinates:

```
List<Placemark> placemarks = await Geolocator().placemarkFromCoordinates(

_currentPosition.latitude,

_currentPosition.longitude,

);

if (placemarks.isNotEmpty) {

Placemark placemark = placemarks.first;

print(placemark.name); // Street name

print(placemark.locality); // City

print(placemark.country); // Country

}
```

Use Cases

The integration of GPS and location services opens up a wide range of use cases for Flutter applications:

- **Mapping and Navigation**: Develop GPS-based mapping and navigation apps for driving, walking, or public transportation.

- **Local Search and Recommendations**: Create apps that provide location-based search results, recommendations, and information about nearby places of interest.

- **Geofencing**: Implement geofencing to trigger events or notifications when a user enters or exits predefined geographic areas.

- **Fitness and Health**: Build fitness and health apps that track and log outdoor activities like running and cycling using GPS data.

- **Location-Aware Social Networking**: Enhance social networking apps with location-based features, such as check-ins and nearby friend notifications.

- **Local Business Services**: Develop apps for local businesses, such as food delivery services, ride-sharing, and booking appointments based on user location.

In conclusion, Flutter's geolocator package simplifies the integration of GPS and location services, making it easier for developers to create location-aware applications. Whether you're building navigation apps, local search services, or location-based social networking, Flutter provides the tools and packages necessary to harness the power of location data in your mobile applications.

Section 15.4: Camera and Media Integration

Flutter's rich ecosystem includes plugins and packages that make it easy to integrate camera and media capabilities into your mobile applications. In this section, we'll explore how to utilize these resources to capture photos and videos, as well as work with multimedia content in your Flutter app.

Camera Plugin

To access device cameras, you can use the camera plugin. This plugin allows you to take photos and record videos using the device's built-in cameras. To get started, add the camera package to your pubspec.yaml file:

```
dependencies:

flutter:

sdk: flutter

camera: ^latest_version
```

After adding the dependency, run flutter pub get to fetch the package.

Capturing Photos

To capture a photo using the device's camera, you can use the camera plugin like this:

```
import 'package:flutter/material.dart';

import 'package:camera/camera.dart';

class CameraScreen extends StatefulWidget {

@override

_CameraScreenState createState() => _CameraScreenState();

}
```

```
class _CameraScreenState extends State<CameraScreen> {
CameraController _controller;
List<CameraDescription> _cameras;
@override
void initState() {
super.initState();
_initializeCamera();
}
void _initializeCamera() async {
_cameras = await availableCameras();
_controller = CameraController(
_cameras[0], // Select the first available camera
ResolutionPreset.medium,
);
await _controller.initialize();
if (!mounted) return;
setState(() {});
}
@override
void dispose() {
```

```
_controller?.dispose();
super.dispose();
}
@override
Widget build(BuildContext context) {
if (!_controller.value.isInitialized) {
return Container();
}
return Scaffold(
appBar: AppBar(
title: Text('Camera Example'),
),
body: CameraPreview(_controller),
floatingActionButton: FloatingActionButton(
onPressed: () async {
try {
final XFile photo = await _controller.takePicture();
// Handle captured photo, e.g., save it or display it
print('Photo saved at ${photo.path}');
} catch (e) {
```

```
print('Error capturing photo: $e');
}
},
child: Icon(Icons.camera),
),
);
}
}
```

In this code, we initialize the camera controller, display the camera preview, and use a floating action button to capture a photo.

Recording Videos

To record videos, you can modify the code as follows:

```
// Inside the _CameraScreenState class
Future<void> _startRecording() async {
try {
final XFile video = await _controller.startVideoRecording();
// Recording started, handle video path
print('Recording video at ${video.path}');
} catch (e) {
print('Error starting video recording: $e');
```

```
}
}
Future<void> _stopRecording() async {
try {
await _controller.stopVideoRecording();
// Recording stopped, handle the recorded video
} catch (e) {
print('Error stopping video recording: $e');
}
}
```

You can call _startRecording to begin recording and _stopRecording to stop recording.

Working with Media

In addition to capturing photos and videos, Flutter offers packages for working with multimedia content:

- **Image Picker**: The image_picker package allows users to select images from their device's gallery or take photos using the camera.
- **Video Player**: The video_player package provides a widget for playing video files.
- **Audio Player**: The audioplayers package enables audio playback and control.

- **Image and Video Processing**: Packages like image, video_thumbnail, and flutter_ffmpeg allow you to process, edit, and manipulate images and videos.

By incorporating these packages into your Flutter app, you can create feature-rich multimedia experiences, from image editing and playback to audio recording and streaming.

In conclusion, Flutter's extensive ecosystem offers everything you need to integrate camera and media functionality seamlessly into your mobile applications. Whether you're building a social media app, a multimedia editor, or a content-sharing platform, Flutter provides the tools and packages to handle photos, videos, and other media content with ease.

Section 15.5: Hardware Acceleration and Performance

Performance optimization is a critical aspect of mobile app development, and Flutter provides various techniques and tools to ensure your app runs smoothly and efficiently on both Android and iOS devices. In this section, we'll explore hardware acceleration, performance best practices, and tools for profiling and debugging to create high-performing Flutter apps.

Hardware Acceleration

Hardware acceleration leverages the device's GPU (Graphics Processing Unit) to offload graphical rendering tasks, leading to improved app performance. Flutter takes advantage of hardware acceleration by default, ensuring that your app's UI is rendered efficiently. However, there are additional ways to optimize hardware usage:

Custom Paint

The CustomPaint widget allows you to create custom graphics and drawings in your app efficiently. By directly manipulating pixels on the screen using the CustomPainter class, you can achieve complex UI effects while benefiting from hardware acceleration. This approach is particularly useful for tasks like animations, chart rendering, and custom widgets.

Flutter's Render Engine

Flutter uses a high-performance rendering engine that optimizes the rendering process by minimizing GPU and CPU usage. The engine takes advantage of hardware acceleration to efficiently redraw only the parts of the screen that have changed, resulting in smooth animations and reduced battery consumption.

Performance Best Practices

To ensure optimal app performance, consider the following best practices:

Minimize Widget Rebuilds

Excessive widget rebuilding can negatively impact performance. Use the const keyword for widgets that don't change and employ tools like const constructors and ValueKey to prevent unnecessary widget rebuilds.

Efficient List Views

For large lists, use widgets like ListView.builder and ListView.separated to create efficient, scrollable lists. These widgets only render items that are visible on the screen, saving memory and improving scrolling performance.

Avoid Expensive Operations in the Build Method

Expensive operations, such as network requests and complex calculations, should be performed outside the build method to prevent blocking the UI thread. Use async/await for asynchronous operations and isolate for compute-intensive tasks.

Asset Optimization

Optimize your assets, such as images and videos, to reduce their size and load times. Consider using compressed formats like WebP for images and efficient video codecs.

Memory Management

Monitor and manage memory usage using Flutter's built-in DevTools or external tools like the Dart Observatory. Detect and address memory leaks and unnecessary object creation.

Profiling and Debugging

Flutter provides powerful tools for profiling and debugging your app's performance:

Flutter DevTools

DevTools is a suite of performance analysis and debugging tools integrated into Flutter. It offers insights into your app's performance, memory usage, and UI layout. DevTools also allows you to profile your app's performance, identify bottlenecks, and optimize your code.

Dart Observatory

The Dart Observatory is a debugging and profiling tool that provides real-time insights into your app's execution, CPU usage, memory allocation, and more. It can help you identify performance issues and memory leaks by analyzing your app's runtime behavior.

Performance Overlay

Flutter's performance overlay is a built-in tool that displays a real-time graph of your app's frame rate and GPU usage directly on the device screen. You can enable it to identify performance bottlenecks during development and testing.

In conclusion, optimizing the performance of your Flutter app is essential for providing a smooth and responsive user experience. By leveraging hardware acceleration, following performance best practices, and utilizing profiling and debugging tools like DevTools and the Dart Observatory, you can ensure that your app runs efficiently on a wide range of devices and delivers a high-quality user experience.

Chapter 16: Flutter for Enterprise

Section 16.1: Implementing Enterprise-Level Features

In the rapidly evolving world of mobile app development, Flutter has emerged as a versatile framework with capabilities that extend far beyond individual and small-scale projects. Enterprises have recognized the potential of Flutter to deliver high-quality, cross-platform applications efficiently. In this section, we will explore how Flutter can be leveraged to implement enterprise-level features and address the unique challenges faced by large organizations.

The Challenges of Enterprise Development

Enterprise-level applications come with a distinct set of challenges. These applications often need to handle a significant amount of data, support complex workflows, and ensure the highest levels of security. Here are some common challenges in enterprise app development:

1. **Scalability**: Enterprise apps must be able to handle a large number of concurrent users and a growing volume of data. Scalability is a critical consideration.
2. **Security**: Enterprises deal with sensitive data, making security a top priority. Robust security measures are essential to protect against data breaches.
3. **Integration**: Enterprise apps often need to integrate with various existing systems, databases, and third-party services. Seamless integration is crucial for efficient operations.
4. **Compliance**: Enterprises are subject to industry-specific regulations and compliance standards. Adhering to these standards is non-negotiable.

5. **Customization**: Different departments and teams within an organization may have unique requirements. Enterprise apps should allow for customization to meet these needs.

Leveraging Flutter for Enterprise Development

Flutter provides several advantages when it comes to addressing these challenges:

- **Cross-Platform**: Flutter's cross-platform nature allows enterprises to develop and maintain a single codebase for both iOS and Android, reducing development time and costs.

- **High Performance**: Flutter's compiled code executes directly on the device's native hardware, ensuring excellent performance.

- **Customization**: Flutter's widget-based architecture makes it easy to create custom UI components and tailor the app to specific requirements.

- **Integration**: Flutter provides plugins and packages for integrating with various backend systems, APIs, and databases, simplifying the integration process.

- **Security**: Flutter follows best practices for security, and its compiled nature reduces the risk of common vulnerabilities.

Use Cases for Enterprise Flutter Apps

Enterprise-level Flutter applications find use in various domains:

- **Customer Relationship Management (CRM)**: Enterprises can develop CRM apps to manage interactions with customers and clients efficiently.

- **Inventory Management**: Flutter apps can streamline inventory tracking, reducing manual efforts and improving accuracy.

- **Human Resources (HR)**: HR departments can benefit from Flutter apps for employee onboarding, leave management, and performance evaluations.

- **Analytics and Reporting**: Enterprises can build reporting tools that provide insights into business data, helping in data-driven decision-making.

- **E-commerce**: Flutter can be used to create robust e-commerce platforms with advanced features like shopping carts, payment gateways, and product catalogs.

In this section, we will delve into the practical aspects of implementing enterprise-level features with Flutter. We will explore case studies, architectural considerations, and best practices to ensure the successful deployment of enterprise Flutter applications. Whether you're a developer working on enterprise projects or a decision-maker considering Flutter for your organization, this section will provide valuable insights into harnessing the power of Flutter in an enterprise context.

Section 16.2: Security and Data Protection

Security is a paramount concern in enterprise app development, and Flutter provides tools and best practices to help developers build secure applications that protect sensitive data. In this section, we will explore various aspects of security and data protection in enterprise Flutter apps.

Data Encryption and Storage

One of the fundamental aspects of security is the protection of data, both at rest and in transit. Flutter provides libraries and packages that can be used to implement encryption for sensitive data stored on the device or transmitted over the network.

For data at rest, the flutter_secure_storage package is commonly used to securely store sensitive information such as API keys, access tokens, and user credentials. This package encrypts the data and stores it in a platform-specific secure storage mechanism, ensuring that it is not easily accessible even if the device is compromised.

When it comes to data in transit, Flutter supports HTTPS for secure communication with remote servers. You can make use of the http package to perform secure HTTP requests. Additionally, for more advanced scenarios, you can implement certificate pinning to ensure that the app communicates only with trusted servers.

Authentication and Authorization

Authentication and authorization are critical components of enterprise app security. Flutter provides various authentication libraries and services that can be integrated into your app to ensure that only authorized users can access sensitive functionality and data.

For user authentication, Firebase Authentication is a popular choice. It offers a range of authentication methods, including email/ password, phone number, and social media logins. Firebase also provides security rules that can be used to define fine-grained access control to Firebase resources.

In cases where more control is required over the authentication process, you can integrate OAuth-based authentication flows using packages like flutter_appauth. This allows you to connect your app to identity providers such as Google, Facebook, or custom OAuth providers.

Authorization can be managed using role-based access control (RBAC) mechanisms. Depending on the architecture of your enterprise app, you can implement RBAC within your backend services or use Firebase's Realtime Database or Firestore to define and enforce access rules.

Secure Communication with APIs

Enterprise apps often need to communicate with backend APIs to access data and services. To ensure secure communication, you can follow best practices such as:

- Implementing API key or token-based authentication.
- Using secure HTTPS connections.
- Validating and sanitizing API responses to protect against data injection attacks.

Compliance and Data Privacy

Many industries have specific compliance requirements related to data privacy and security, such as GDPR in Europe or HIPAA in the healthcare sector. Flutter allows developers to build apps that can comply with these regulations by providing tools for data encryption, secure storage, and user consent management.

When dealing with sensitive user data, it's essential to inform users about data collection and obtain their consent where necessary. Flutter's consent_package and custom dialogs can be used to create user-friendly consent flows.

Ongoing Security Maintenance

Security is an ongoing process, and it's essential to regularly update your enterprise Flutter app to address security vulnerabilities and stay ahead of emerging threats. Stay informed about security best practices, security releases of Flutter and its dependencies, and conduct regular security audits and penetration testing.

In conclusion, Flutter offers robust support for security and data protection, making it a suitable choice for enterprise app development. By implementing encryption, secure communication, authentication, and authorization mechanisms, you can build enterprise apps that meet the highest security standards and protect sensitive data from threats and unauthorized access.

Section 16.3: Flutter in a Corporate Environment

Flutter has gained popularity not only among independent developers and startups but also within corporate environments. Its ability to create beautiful and performant cross-platform apps with a single codebase has made it an attractive choice for companies looking to streamline their app development efforts. In this section, we will explore the use of Flutter in a corporate context.

Benefits of Flutter in Corporate Settings

1. Cost-Efficiency

One of the primary reasons corporations adopt Flutter is cost-efficiency. Developing separate apps for iOS and Android can be resource-intensive, but Flutter allows companies to maintain a single codebase for both platforms, reducing development and maintenance costs.

2. Faster Development

Flutter's "write once, run anywhere" philosophy accelerates app development. Corporate teams can release products faster and respond to market demands promptly. The hot-reload feature significantly shortens the development cycle and allows for quick iterations.

3. Consistency Across Platforms

Maintaining a consistent user experience across different platforms is crucial for corporate apps. Flutter's widget-based architecture and rich set of customizable widgets ensure that the app's look and feel remains consistent, enhancing brand identity.

4. Productivity

Corporate developers can leverage their existing programming skills, such as knowledge of the Dart programming language or experience with object-oriented programming, to transition into Flutter development seamlessly. This familiarity leads to increased productivity.

5. Access to Native Features

Flutter's robust plugin system provides access to native device features and APIs. Corporate apps often require integration with device-specific functionalities, and Flutter's plugins simplify this process.

Use Cases for Corporate Apps

1. Internal Tools and Dashboards

Corporations use Flutter to build internal tools, dashboards, and productivity-enhancing apps. These apps help streamline operations, automate tasks, and provide employees with efficient tools for their day-to-day work.

2. Customer-Facing Apps

Many corporations develop customer-facing apps to enhance the user experience, offer self-service features, and improve customer engagement. Flutter's ability to deliver a consistent user experience across platforms is advantageous in this regard.

3. Field Workforce Apps

Corporations with field service teams or a mobile workforce rely on Flutter to build apps for job scheduling, data collection, and reporting. These apps often require integration with device sensors and offline capabilities, which Flutter supports.

4. Training and Education

Flutter is used to create training and educational apps for employees and customers. Its interactive and visually appealing UI capabilities make it suitable for e-learning solutions.

5. Enterprise Resource Planning (ERP)

Large corporations implement Flutter to build ERP solutions, which integrate various business processes and functions into a single platform. Flutter's ability to create custom UI components is advantageous for ERP apps.

Challenges and Considerations

While Flutter offers numerous advantages, corporations must also consider potential challenges:

1. Integration with Existing Systems

Integrating Flutter apps with existing corporate systems, databases, and APIs may require additional development effort. Compatibility and data synchronization need careful consideration.

2. Security and Compliance

Corporate apps often handle sensitive data and must adhere to security and compliance standards. Thorough security testing and compliance checks are essential.

3. Long-Term Support

Corporations need to assess Flutter's long-term support and the availability of Flutter developers to ensure the sustainability of their apps.

In summary, Flutter is gaining traction in corporate environments due to its cost-efficiency, development speed, and cross-platform capabilities. Its use cases span a wide range of corporate needs, from internal tools to customer-facing apps. However, careful consideration of integration, security, and long-term support is necessary for a successful Flutter adoption within the corporate ecosystem.

Section 16.4: Case Studies: Flutter in Large-Scale Projects

Flutter's ability to handle complex and large-scale projects has made it a popular choice among organizations tackling ambitious software development initiatives. In this section, we will explore case studies of large-scale projects that have successfully utilized Flutter.

1. Alibaba: Super App Redesign

Alibaba, one of the world's largest e-commerce companies, embarked on a project to redesign their Super App, which serves millions of users. They chose Flutter to modernize their app's user interface and improve performance. By using Flutter, Alibaba achieved a consistent and visually appealing user experience across Android and iOS devices. The app's responsiveness and fast development cycle allowed Alibaba to iterate quickly and meet user expectations.

2. Tencent: Qingyan

Tencent, a technology conglomerate, developed the Qingyan app using Flutter. Qingyan is a comprehensive digital marketing platform that provides a range of services, including data analysis, ad management, and content creation. Flutter's ability to create a customized user interface and its excellent performance were crucial factors in Tencent's choice. The app's cross-platform nature enabled Tencent to reach a broad user base efficiently.

3. Square: Square Register

Square, a payment processing company, utilized Flutter to build its Square Register app. This point-of-sale (POS) application is used by businesses for payment processing, inventory management, and sales tracking. Flutter's ability to create a consistent and visually appealing user interface was essential for Square, as it ensures that businesses using the app maintain a professional image.

4. BMW: BMW Connected

BMW, a renowned automotive manufacturer, implemented Flutter in their BMW Connected app. This app allows BMW owners to control various vehicle functions remotely, access service information, and interact with the car's infotainment system. Flutter's cross-platform capabilities allowed BMW to offer the same features and user experience to both Android and iOS users.

5. Huawei: Huawei AppGallery

Huawei, a global technology company, used Flutter to develop the Huawei AppGallery app store. This app serves as the primary platform for users to discover and download apps on Huawei devices. Flutter's efficiency in creating a rich and consistent user interface was crucial for Huawei in providing a seamless app discovery experience to its users.

6. Reflectly: A Mindfulness Journal

Reflectly, a popular mindfulness and journaling app, switched to Flutter to improve app performance and maintain a consistent look across platforms. By adopting Flutter, Reflectly was able to streamline development and ensure that users on both Android and iOS devices received a visually cohesive experience. The app's success highlights Flutter's potential for consumer-facing applications.

7. Groupon: Merchant App

Groupon, a global e-commerce marketplace, used Flutter to build its Merchant app. This app empowers businesses to manage their Groupon deals, track customer redemptions, and access sales analytics. Flutter's development efficiency allowed Groupon to provide an intuitive and feature-rich experience to its merchant partners.

These case studies demonstrate that Flutter is not only capable of handling large-scale projects but can also provide benefits such as development speed, visual consistency, and cross-platform capabilities. Organizations across various industries have leveraged Flutter to create successful applications that cater to diverse user bases. The adoption of Flutter in such projects highlights its suitability for ambitious software development initiatives.

Section 16.5: Future Trends in Enterprise Mobile Development

The landscape of enterprise mobile development is continually evolving, driven by emerging technologies and changing business needs. In this section, we'll explore some future trends that are expected to shape enterprise mobile development, including how Flutter and Dart are likely to play a role in these developments.

1. Increased Emphasis on Cross-Platform Development

Enterprise organizations are increasingly recognizing the advantages of cross-platform development for mobile apps. The ability to write code once and deploy it on multiple platforms not only reduces development costs but also accelerates time-to-market. Flutter, with its cross-platform capabilities, is poised to gain even more prominence as organizations seek to maximize efficiency.

2. Integration with Augmented Reality (AR) and Virtual Reality (VR)

As AR and VR technologies become more accessible and mature, enterprise mobile apps will explore ways to integrate these technologies into their workflows. Flutter's extensibility and ability to work with custom plugins make it a candidate for building AR and VR experiences within apps for training, simulation, and visualization purposes.

3. Enhanced Security Measures

With the increasing importance of mobile apps in handling sensitive data and transactions, security remains a top priority for enterprises. Future trends will likely include stronger encryption, biometric authentication, and secure data storage. Dart, as a language that emphasizes strong typing and asynchronous programming, can help developers create more secure mobile applications.

4. Internet of Things (IoT) Integration

The proliferation of IoT devices presents opportunities for enterprises to connect and control these devices through mobile apps. Flutter's versatility and ability to work with various communication protocols make it suitable for building apps that interact with IoT devices in sectors such as healthcare, manufacturing, and smart homes.

5. Artificial Intelligence (AI) and Machine Learning (ML)

AI and ML are expected to play an increasingly significant role in enterprise mobile apps. These technologies can provide data-driven insights, personalization, and automation of tasks. Dart's compatibility with TensorFlow, Google's open-source machine learning framework, positions it as a valuable tool for building AI and ML-powered apps.

6. Progressive Web Apps (PWAs) and Flutter for Web

PWAs offer the benefits of both web and mobile apps, providing offline access, fast loading times, and cross-platform compatibility. Flutter for Web, an emerging technology, will enable developers to create web applications using Flutter, further blurring the lines between web and mobile development.

7. Enhanced User Experience

User experience (UX) will continue to be a focal point for enterprise apps. Flutter's capabilities in creating beautiful and responsive UIs, along with its support for animations and custom designs, will be instrumental in delivering superior user experiences that meet the expectations of modern users.

8. Localization and Globalization

As businesses expand globally, mobile apps will need to cater to diverse audiences. Flutter's internationalization and localization features will become increasingly important for enterprises aiming to reach users in different regions with tailored content and experiences.

In conclusion, the future of enterprise mobile development holds exciting prospects, and Flutter and Dart are well-positioned to thrive in this evolving landscape. Their flexibility, performance, and support for cutting-edge technologies make them valuable tools for developers and organizations looking to stay at the forefront of mobile app development for enterprises. By keeping an eye on these emerging trends and leveraging the capabilities of Flutter and Dart, enterprises can develop innovative and successful mobile solutions.

Section 17.1: Engaging with the Flutter Community

The Flutter community is a vibrant and welcoming ecosystem that plays a crucial role in the success and growth of Flutter and Dart. Engaging with the community can be highly beneficial for developers, whether they are beginners or experienced professionals. In this section, we will explore the various aspects of the Flutter community, why it's important, and how you can get involved.

Why Engage with the Flutter Community?

Engaging with the Flutter community offers several advantages:

1. **Learning and Skill Improvement:** The community provides a wealth of resources, including tutorials, articles, and open-source projects. By participating, you can

enhance your skills and stay up-to-date with the latest developments in Flutter and Dart.

2. **Problem Solving:** When you encounter challenges or bugs in your projects, the community can be an invaluable source of solutions. You can seek help, share your knowledge, and collaborate with others to resolve issues more efficiently.
3. **Networking and Collaboration:** Building connections with fellow Flutter developers can lead to collaboration opportunities, job offers, and partnerships. It's a chance to work on exciting projects together and grow your professional network.
4. **Contribution:** Contributing to open-source projects or the Flutter framework itself is a rewarding experience. It allows you to give back to the community and have a positive impact on the ecosystem.

Ways to Engage with the Flutter Community

Here are some effective ways to engage with the Flutter community:

1. **Online Forums:** Participate in online forums such as the Flutter Dev Google Group and Flutter Community on Reddit to ask questions, share knowledge, and connect with developers.
2. **Flutter Packages:** Explore and contribute to packages on pub.dev[1], the official package repository for Flutter. You can create your packages or improve existing ones.
3. **GitHub:** Get involved in open-source projects related to Flutter and Dart on GitHub by submitting bug reports, feature requests, or pull requests.
4. **Social Media:** Follow Flutter and Dart-related accounts

1. https://pub.dev/

on platforms like Twitter, LinkedIn, and Instagram. Engage in discussions, share your projects, and learn from others.

5. **Flutter Meetups and Conferences:** Attend local Flutter meetups and conferences to network with developers in person. These events often feature talks, workshops, and opportunities to showcase your work.
6. **Blogging and Tutorials:** Share your knowledge and experiences through blog posts, tutorials, and YouTube videos. This not only helps others but also establishes you as an authority in the field.
7. **Contribute to Documentation:** Help improve the official Flutter and Dart documentation to make it more accessible and comprehensive for developers.
8. **Hackathons and Challenges:** Participate in Flutter-related hackathons and coding challenges to test your skills and potentially win prizes.
9. **Mentoring:** Consider becoming a mentor or seeking mentorship within the community. Mentoring can be a fulfilling way to learn and grow together.
10. **Local Communities:** Join or create local Flutter communities or user groups to connect with developers in your area.

Code of Conduct and Etiquette

While engaging with the Flutter community, it's essential to follow the Flutter Community Code of Conduct to ensure a respectful and inclusive environment for all members. Treat others with kindness, patience, and empathy, and remember that diversity is one of the community's strengths.

In conclusion, the Flutter community is a valuable resource for developers interested in Flutter and Dart. Engaging with the community can accelerate your learning, provide solutions to problems, and open doors to exciting opportunities in mobile app development. Whether you're a newcomer or an experienced developer, actively participating in the community can enhance your journey in the world of Flutter and Dart.

Section 17.2: Contributing to Open Source Projects

Contributing to open-source projects is a meaningful way to give back to the Flutter and Dart community while honing your skills and gaining valuable experience. In this section, we'll explore the process of contributing to open source and provide guidance on how you can get started.

Why Contribute to Open Source?

Contributing to open-source projects offers several benefits:

1. **Skill Development:** Open source exposes you to a wide range of programming challenges. By tackling issues and collaborating with experienced developers, you can improve your coding skills.
2. **Resume Enhancement:** Open-source contributions are a valuable addition to your resume. They demonstrate your ability to work on real-world projects and collaborate within a development community.
3. **Community Engagement:** Being an active contributor allows you to interact with other developers, learn from their expertise, and build professional relationships.
4. **Giving Back:** Open source relies on the contributions of

volunteers. By contributing, you help improve tools and libraries that benefit the entire community.

Finding Open Source Projects

To get started, you need to find open-source projects related to Flutter and Dart that align with your interests and expertise. Here are some resources to help you find projects:

1. **GitHub:** Explore the Flutter GitHub organization and Dart GitHub organization to discover official projects and related repositories.
2. **Package Repositories:** Visit pub.dev[2] for Dart packages and pub.dev/flutter for Flutter packages. You can find open-source packages and libraries to contribute to.
3. **Community Forums:** Check Flutter and Dart community forums, such as the Flutter Dev Google Group and Dart Discussion Google Group, for project announcements and requests for contributions.

Steps to Contribute

Once you've identified a project you'd like to contribute to, follow these general steps:

1. **Familiarize Yourself:** Read the project's documentation, contributing guidelines, and code of conduct. Understand the project's goals and how it operates.
2. **Select an Issue:** Look for issues labeled as "good first issue" or "beginner-friendly." These are typically suitable for newcomers.
3. **Claim the Issue:** Comment on the issue to express your interest in working on it. The maintainers will often assign

2. https://pub.dev/

the issue to you.

4. **Set Up Your Development Environment:** Follow the project's instructions for setting up your development environment. This may involve installing dependencies, configuring tools, and cloning the repository.
5. **Create a Branch:** Create a new branch for your contribution. Branch names often follow a convention like "fix/issue-number" or "feature/descriptive-name."
6. **Write Code:** Implement the necessary changes or fixes following the project's coding style and guidelines.
7. **Tests and Documentation:** Ensure your code includes tests, and update documentation if necessary.
8. **Submit a Pull Request (PR):** Push your changes to your branch and submit a PR to the project's repository. Describe your changes, reference the issue, and wait for feedback.
9. **Address Feedback:** Be prepared to address feedback from project maintainers. Collaborate with them to improve your contribution.
10. **Review and Merge:** Once your PR is approved, it will be reviewed by maintainers. After any final adjustments, it may be merged into the project.

Etiquette and Best Practices

When contributing to open source, it's essential to follow some etiquette and best practices:

1. **Respect Project Guidelines:** Adhere to the project's coding style, testing practices, and documentation standards.
2. **Stay Engaged:** Respond promptly to comments and feedback on your PR. Collaboration and communication

are key.

3. **Be Patient:** Understand that maintainers and reviewers may have limited time. Be patient while waiting for responses.
4. **Ask for Help:** If you're unsure about something, don't hesitate to ask for guidance. The community is usually willing to help.
5. **Contribute Regularly:** Consider making contributions regularly. This helps you build a reputation within the community.
6. **Be Courteous:** Maintain a respectful and professional tone in your interactions with others.

In conclusion, contributing to open source projects related to Flutter and Dart is a valuable way to enhance your skills, engage with the community, and give back to the ecosystem. By following best practices, respecting project guidelines, and staying engaged, you can make meaningful contributions that benefit both you and the broader developer community.

Section 17.3: Leveraging Community Resources and Libraries

One of the strengths of the Flutter and Dart ecosystems is the vibrant and supportive community. In this section, we'll explore how to leverage community resources and libraries to enhance your Flutter and Dart projects.

The Power of Community Resources

The Flutter and Dart communities offer a wealth of resources that can significantly accelerate your development process. Here are some key community resources to be aware of:

1. **Official Documentation:** The official Flutter and Dart documentation is an invaluable resource. It provides comprehensive guides, APIs, and examples to help you understand and use the frameworks effectively. Always start here when you have questions.
2. **Community Forums:** Platforms like Flutter Dev Google Group and Dart Discussion Google Group serve as forums for discussions and problem-solving. You can ask questions, share your experiences, and learn from others.
3. **GitHub:** GitHub hosts countless open-source Flutter and Dart projects. You can find libraries, packages, and sample apps that can save you time and effort. Be sure to check the repository's README and documentation for usage instructions.
4. **Pub.dev:** Pub.dev is the official package repository for Dart. You can discover, download, and publish Dart packages here. It's a treasure trove of libraries that can help you with various tasks.
5. **Flutter Community:** The Flutter Community[3] website is a curated collection of Flutter packages and resources. It provides easy access to a wide range of packages, making it easier to find the right tools for your project.
6. **Stack Overflow:** Stack Overflow is a popular platform for asking and answering programming questions. Both Flutter and Dart have active communities on Stack Overflow. You can search for solutions to common problems or ask your questions.
7. **Medium and Blogs:** Many developers and experts in the Flutter and Dart community share their knowledge through blogs, articles, and tutorials on platforms like Medium. These articles can offer insights, tips, and best

3. https://fluttercommunity.dev/

practices.

Leveraging Libraries and Packages

Using existing libraries and packages can save you a significant amount of development time. When choosing a library, consider factors like community support, maintenance, and compatibility with your project's requirements. Here's how to incorporate libraries into your Flutter or Dart project:

1. **Dependency Management:** In your project's pubspec.yaml file, specify the dependencies you need. Flutter uses the dependencies section, while Dart packages use the dependencies section in the same way.

dependencies:

flutter:

sdk: flutter

http: ^latest_version

1. **Version Constraints:** You can specify version constraints to ensure your project uses compatible versions of packages. Use the ^ symbol to indicate that your project is compatible with the specified version and its compatible updates.
2. **Package Installation:** Run flutter pub get to fetch and install the specified packages. For Dart, you can use pub get.
3. **Importing Packages:** Import the package in your Dart code using the import statement.

import 'package:http/http.dart' as http;

1. **Usage:** You can now use the library's functionality in your code. Refer to the library's documentation and examples for guidance on usage.
2. **Maintenance:** Keep your packages up to date by periodically running flutter pub upgrade or pub upgrade. This ensures you have access to bug fixes and new features.

Contributing to the Community

If you find a library or package particularly useful, consider contributing back to the community. You can contribute by:

1. **Reporting Issues:** If you encounter bugs or issues with a library, report them on the project's GitHub repository. Provide detailed information to help maintainers understand and fix the problem.
2. **Contribute Code:** If you're comfortable with the library's codebase, you can contribute by fixing issues, adding new features, or improving documentation. Fork the repository, make your changes, and submit a pull request.
3. **Documentation:** Improving documentation by fixing typos, clarifying explanations, or providing usage examples can be a valuable contribution.
4. **Support Others:** Answer questions on community forums like Stack Overflow or help fellow developers who are struggling with a particular library.

By leveraging community resources, libraries, and contributing to the ecosystem, you not only enhance your own projects but also contribute to the growth and strength of the Flutter and Dart communities. It's a win-win situation that fosters collaboration and innovation.

Section 17.4: Hosting and Participating in Hackathons

Participating in hackathons is an excellent way to apply your Flutter and Dart skills, learn from others, and potentially collaborate on exciting projects. In this section, we'll explore the world of hackathons, how to participate, and even host one if you're up for the challenge.

What Is a Hackathon?

A hackathon is an event where individuals or teams come together to create software projects within a limited time frame, typically 24 to 48 hours. The goal is to build functional and innovative solutions to specific challenges or problems. Hackathons can focus on various themes, including mobile app development, web development, hardware integration, and more.

Why Participate in a Hackathon?

Participating in a hackathon offers several benefits:

1. **Skill Enhancement:** Hackathons provide a platform to apply your Flutter and Dart skills in a real-world setting. You can work on new and challenging projects, expanding your knowledge and capabilities.
2. **Collaboration:** Hackathons often involve teamwork, allowing you to collaborate with other developers, designers, and domain experts. Collaborative experiences can be incredibly valuable.

3. **Innovation:** The time constraints and competitive nature of hackathons encourage innovative thinking. You might come up with creative solutions that you wouldn't have considered otherwise.
4. **Networking:** Hackathons are an excellent opportunity to network with fellow developers, mentors, and potential employers. Building connections in the tech industry can open doors to future opportunities.
5. **Prizes and Recognition:** Many hackathons offer prizes, recognition, and opportunities for your project to be showcased. Winning or even participating can be a valuable addition to your portfolio.

How to Participate

Participating in a hackathon involves a few key steps:

1. **Find Hackathons:** Look for hackathons that align with your interests and skills. You can find hackathon listings on websites like Devpost, HackerRank, and ChallengePost.
2. **Register:** Sign up for the hackathon through the provided registration process. Pay attention to any eligibility criteria or team size limits.
3. **Prepare:** Before the hackathon, prepare by setting up your development environment, gathering any necessary tools or libraries, and brainstorming project ideas.
4. **Form a Team:** If it's a team-based hackathon and you don't already have a team, you can often find teammates through hackathon platforms or forums.
5. **Attend the Hackathon:** On the day of the hackathon, attend the opening ceremonies or kickoff events. Listen to the challenge presentations and any rules or guidelines.
6. **Build Your Project:** Use your Flutter and Dart skills to

develop your project within the specified time frame. Focus on creating a working prototype or demo.

7. **Seek Help:** Don't hesitate to ask mentors or organizers for help if you encounter technical issues or need guidance.
8. **Submit Your Project:** Once your project is ready, submit it according to the hackathon's submission process. Include a project description, demo, and any additional requirements.
9. **Present Your Project:** If required, present your project to judges or attendees. Be prepared to explain your solution and its significance.
10. **Enjoy the Experience:** Hackathons are not only about winning but also about the experience. Enjoy the opportunity to learn, collaborate, and innovate.

Hosting Your Own Hackathon

If you have the expertise and resources, hosting your hackathon can be a rewarding endeavor. Here are some steps to consider:

1. **Define the Purpose:** Determine the goals, themes, and challenges of your hackathon. What do you want participants to achieve?
2. **Plan Logistics:** Organize the event logistics, including the date, location (physical or virtual), duration, and any prizes or sponsorship arrangements.
3. **Create Rules:** Establish clear rules and guidelines for participants, including eligibility criteria, judging criteria, and code of conduct.
4. **Registration:** Set up a registration process and a platform for participants to sign up. Ensure that you have a system for team formation if it's a team-based hackathon.
5. **Promotion:** Promote your hackathon through various

channels, including social media, tech communities, and relevant forums. Reach out to potential sponsors.

6. **Provide Resources:** Make development resources, APIs, libraries, and mentors available to participants to support their projects.
7. **Judging and Prizes:** Assemble a panel of judges with expertise in the field. Define how projects will be evaluated and determine the prizes or recognition for winners.
8. **Execution:** Run the hackathon smoothly, ensuring that participants have access to the necessary tools and support.
9. **Submission and Evaluation:** Set up a submission platform for participants to submit their projects. Ensure that judging is fair and unbiased.
10. **Closing and Celebration:** Conclude the hackathon with a closing ceremony where winners are announced, and participants have an opportunity to showcase their projects.

Hosting a hackathon can be a significant undertaking, but it can also foster a sense of community, encourage innovation, and provide exposure to emerging talent.

Conclusion

Hackathons

Section 17.5: Learning from Flutter Success Stories

Learning from success stories within the Flutter community can provide valuable insights, inspiration, and guidance for your own Flutter journey. In this section, we'll explore some notable Flutter success stories and the key takeaways they offer.

Success Story 1: Alibaba

Alibaba, one of the world's largest e-commerce companies, adopted Flutter for their mobile app development needs. They utilized Flutter to enhance the user experience and improve performance across different platforms. Alibaba's success with Flutter highlights its capability to handle large-scale, real-world applications.

Key Takeaways:

- Flutter's cross-platform nature makes it a suitable choice for organizations with diverse user bases.
- Improved app performance and responsiveness can lead to higher user engagement and satisfaction.
- Large enterprises can benefit from Flutter's development efficiency and code sharing capabilities.

Success Story 2: Reflectly

Reflectly, a popular journaling app, saw significant growth and success after migrating to Flutter. They achieved a consistent and visually appealing user interface across iOS and Android, resulting in increased user retention and positive reviews.

Key Takeaways:

- Flutter's UI consistency across platforms can lead to improved user satisfaction and retention.
- Smaller development teams can benefit from Flutter's productivity and faster time-to-market.

- Migrating to Flutter can breathe new life into existing apps and attract new users.

Success Story 3: Groupon

Groupon, a renowned online marketplace, embraced Flutter for its consumer and merchant apps. Flutter allowed Groupon to maintain a single codebase while delivering a polished and performant experience to both iOS and Android users.

Key Takeaways:

- Maintaining a single codebase simplifies development, reduces costs, and minimizes code duplication.

- Flutter's flexibility and customizability enable companies to adapt their apps to evolving business needs.

- Consistent design and user experience can help establish a strong brand identity.

Success Story 4: eBay Motors

eBay Motors, a marketplace for automotive parts and accessories, adopted Flutter to build a cross-platform solution. By doing so, they reduced development time, ensured consistency, and reached a wider audience.

Key Takeaways:

- Flutter's ability to support custom design and complex interfaces is beneficial for niche markets and specific user needs.

- Time savings from cross-platform development can be redirected to optimizing user experiences and adding new features.

- Reaching a broader audience through multiple platforms can lead to increased revenue opportunities.

Success Story 5: Watermaniac

Watermaniac, a mobile app designed to encourage water consumption, leveraged Flutter's capabilities to create an engaging and user-friendly experience. The app's success demonstrates how Flutter can be applied to various niches and industries.

Key Takeaways:

- Flutter's rich library of pre-built widgets can expedite app development, even for unique concepts.

- User-friendly and visually appealing designs can increase user engagement and app adoption.

- Small startups and independent developers can utilize Flutter to bring innovative ideas to life.

Conclusion

These success stories underscore the versatility and effectiveness of Flutter in real-world scenarios. Whether you're working on a global e-commerce platform, a personal project, or a niche app, Flutter's cross-platform capabilities, consistent UI, and development efficiency can empower you to achieve your goals and deliver exceptional user experiences. By learning from these success stories, you can draw inspiration and guidance as you embark on your own Flutter projects and endeavors.

Chapter 18: Monetization Strategies

Section 18.1: In-App Purchases and Subscriptions

Monetization is a crucial aspect of app development, as it determines how you can generate revenue from your Flutter app. In this section, we will focus on one of the most common monetization strategies: in-app purchases and subscriptions. We'll explore how you can implement these strategies in your Flutter app and make them work effectively.

Understanding In-App Purchases

In-app purchases involve selling digital goods or features within your app. These could be premium content, virtual items, or additional features that enhance the user experience. In Flutter, you can implement in-app purchases using plugins like in_app_purchase.

To get started with in-app purchases, follow these steps:

1. **Set Up Billing Library**: First, you need to integrate the billing library for both Android and iOS. For Android, you'll use Google Play Billing, and for iOS, you'll use StoreKit.
2. **Configure Products**: Define the products you want to sell within your app. These products should be set up in the respective developer consoles (Google Play Console for Android and App Store Connect for iOS).
3. **Implement Purchase Flow**: Create a user-friendly interface for purchasing products. Use the in_app_purchase plugin to fetch available products and initiate the purchase flow when a user decides to buy.

4. **Handle Purchases**: Once a purchase is successful, you'll receive a purchase token. You should validate this token on your server to prevent fraud and ensure the transaction's legitimacy.
5. **Unlock Content**: After a successful purchase, unlock the purchased content or features for the user.

Implementing Subscriptions

Subscriptions are a variation of in-app purchases that allow users to access premium content or features for a recurring fee. For example, you can offer monthly or yearly subscriptions to your users.

To implement subscriptions in your Flutter app:

1. **Configure Subscription Products**: Similar to in-app purchases, configure subscription products in the developer consoles. Define the pricing tiers and billing intervals (e.g., monthly, yearly).
2. **Integrate Billing Libraries**: Ensure you have integrated the billing libraries for Android and iOS.
3. **Offer Subscription Plans**: Create a subscription page in your app where users can choose a subscription plan based on their preferences.
4. **Handle Subscription Logic**: When a user purchases a subscription, your app should handle the subscription logic, such as granting access to premium content and setting up renewal reminders.
5. **Manage Subscriptions**: Keep track of active subscriptions and provide users with options to manage their subscriptions, such as canceling or changing plans.

Best Practices for In-App Purchases and Subscriptions

Here are some best practices to consider when implementing in-app purchases and subscriptions:

- **Transparent Pricing**: Clearly communicate the pricing and benefits of in-app purchases and subscriptions to users. Avoid hidden charges or misleading information.
- **Free Trials**: Offer free trial periods for subscriptions to give users a taste of premium features before committing to a purchase.
- **Localized Pricing**: Consider regional pricing to make your app more accessible to users in different countries.
- **Graceful Handling of Failed Payments**: Handle failed payments gracefully and notify users to update their payment information to avoid service interruptions.
- **User Privacy**: Ensure compliance with privacy regulations and protect user data, especially when handling payments.
- **Subscription Management**: Provide users with easy ways to manage their subscriptions, including cancellation options.

In-app purchases and subscriptions can be effective monetization strategies for your Flutter app, allowing you to generate revenue while providing value to your users. However, it's essential to implement these strategies thoughtfully, with a focus on user experience and transparency.

Section 18.2: Advertisements and Sponsorships

Another common monetization strategy for Flutter apps is incorporating advertisements and sponsorships. These methods allow you to earn revenue by displaying ads within your app or by partnering with sponsors to promote their products or services. In this section, we'll explore how to effectively integrate advertisements and sponsorships into your Flutter app.

Implementing Advertisements

Using Ad Networks

To display advertisements in your app, you can leverage various ad networks such as Google AdMob, Facebook Audience Network, or other third-party ad providers. Here's how you can get started with integrating ads:

1. **Choose an Ad Network**: Select an ad network that suits your app and target audience. Sign up for an account and create ad units.
2. **Add Dependencies**: Include the necessary Flutter plugins and dependencies for the chosen ad network in your app's pubspec.yaml file.
3. **Initialize Advertisements**: Initialize the ad network in your app, typically in the main.dart file. This includes configuring ad units and loading ads.
4. **Display Ads**: Create widgets within your app's UI where ads will be displayed. You can use dedicated ad widgets provided by the plugin or build custom ad integrations.
5. **Ad Monetization**: You'll earn revenue based on impressions, clicks, or conversions generated through the

displayed ads. Ad networks usually provide analytics and payment reports.

Types of Ads

There are various types of ads you can integrate into your app:

- **Banner Ads**: These are small, rectangular ads typically displayed at the top or bottom of the screen. They are less intrusive and can be used in various app screens.

- **Interstitial Ads**: Interstitial ads are full-screen ads that appear at natural transition points in your app, such as between levels in a game or after the completion of an article in a news app.

- **Rewarded Ads**: Rewarded ads offer users a reward, such as in-app currency or an extra life, in exchange for watching a video or engaging with the ad.

- **Native Ads**: Native ads blend seamlessly with your app's content, providing a more integrated user experience. They are often styled to match the app's UI.

Implementing Sponsorships

Sponsorships involve partnering with companies or brands to promote their products or services within your app. Here's how you can integrate sponsorships:

1. **Identify Potential Sponsors**: Find companies or brands that align with your app's audience and content. Reach out to them with sponsorship proposals.
2. **Proposal and Agreement**: Create a proposal outlining the

terms of the sponsorship, including the type and duration of promotion, compensation, and any specific requirements.
3. **Promotion Integration**: Implement the sponsor's promotion within your app. This could include sponsored content, banners, or dedicated sections.
4. **Monitoring and Reporting**: Monitor the performance of the sponsorship and provide reports to sponsors. This helps build trust and maintain long-term partnerships.
5. **Legal Considerations**: Ensure compliance with legal and ethical standards, including disclosure of sponsored content to users.

Balancing User Experience

While advertisements and sponsorships can generate revenue, it's crucial to strike a balance between monetization and user experience. Excessive or intrusive ads can lead to user dissatisfaction and app abandonment. Consider factors such as ad placement, frequency, and relevance to ensure a positive user experience.

By effectively implementing advertisements and sponsorships while prioritizing user satisfaction, you can monetize your Flutter app successfully while maintaining a loyal user base.

Section 18.3: Freemium and Paid App Strategies

In addition to advertisements and sponsorships, freemium and paid app strategies offer alternative ways to monetize your Flutter app. These models involve charging users for access to certain features or content within the app. Let's explore how these strategies work and how to implement them effectively.

Freemium Model

The freemium model, a combination of "free" and "premium," allows users to download your app for free, but offers premium features or content for a fee. This approach enables you to attract a broad user base while generating revenue from users willing to pay for enhanced functionality or exclusive content. Here's how to implement the freemium model:

1. **Core Features for Free**: Provide essential features of your app for free to entice users to download and use it.
2. **Premium Features**: Identify valuable features, content, or functionalities that would enhance the user experience or convenience. These become the "premium" offerings.
3. **In-App Purchases (IAPs)**: Implement in-app purchases to unlock premium features. Flutter provides plugins and packages to manage IAPs, including the in_app_purchase package.
4. **Trial Periods**: Offer trial periods for premium features to give users a taste of what they're missing. After the trial, they can choose to purchase or continue with the free version.
5. **Promotions**: Periodically run promotions or discounts on premium features to incentivize users to upgrade.
6. **User Education**: Clearly communicate the value of premium features to users through in-app messages, tutorials, or feature previews.

Paid App Model

In the paid app model, users are required to purchase your app before downloading it. This model is straightforward but may limit your initial user acquisition. Here's how to implement the paid app model:

1. **App Pricing**: Determine an appropriate price for your app based on its features, uniqueness, and market demand. You can choose a one-time purchase price or offer tiered pricing.
2. **App Store Setup**: Configure your app's pricing and availability on app stores like the Apple App Store and Google Play Store. Ensure users are aware of the price before downloading.
3. **Trial Versions**: Some app stores allow you to offer a limited-time trial version of your app. This allows users to try the app before purchasing the full version.
4. **Demo Videos and Screenshots**: Create compelling demo videos and screenshots on your app store listings to showcase the app's features and functionality.
5. **Regular Updates**: Continuously update your app to improve its value and maintain user satisfaction, encouraging positive reviews and recommendations.

Choosing the Right Model

Deciding between the freemium and paid app models depends on your app's nature and goals. Freemium models are suitable for apps with clear premium features that can enhance user experience. Paid app models are ideal for apps offering substantial value upfront or targeting niche markets.

Whichever model you choose, user experience should remain a top priority. Ensure that both free and premium users have a seamless and enjoyable experience within your app. Providing excellent customer support and timely updates can also foster user loyalty and positive reviews.

Monetizing your Flutter app through freemium or paid models can be a sustainable strategy if executed effectively and aligned with your target audience's preferences and expectations.

Section 18.4: Crowdfunding and Patronage

Crowdfunding and patronage are innovative ways to fund your Flutter app's development and maintenance. These methods rely on the support of a community of backers or patrons who believe in your project's value. In this section, we'll explore how to leverage crowdfunding and patronage effectively.

Crowdfunding

Crowdfunding platforms like Kickstarter, Indiegogo, and Patreon allow you to raise funds for your app by showcasing your project to potential backers. Here's how to use crowdfunding for your Flutter app:

1. **Project Planning**: Define your app's concept, features, and goals. Create a compelling story around your app to attract backers.
2. **Platform Selection**: Choose a suitable crowdfunding platform based on your project's nature. Kickstarter and Indiegogo are popular for raising initial development funds, while Patreon is great for ongoing support.
3. **Campaign Creation**: Create an engaging campaign page that highlights your app's uniqueness, benefits, and development roadmap. Include visuals, videos, and detailed information.

4. **Reward Tiers**: Offer enticing rewards to backers at different tiers. Rewards can include early access, exclusive content, personalized features, or merchandise related to your app.
5. **Promotion**: Promote your campaign through social media, email newsletters, and your app's website. Engage with potential backers, answer questions, and share updates regularly.
6. **Transparency**: Be transparent about your app's progress and how the funds will be used. Building trust with backers is crucial.
7. **Fulfillment**: Deliver rewards promptly as promised. Failure to do so can harm your reputation and future crowdfunding efforts.

Patronage

Patronage is a modern take on the traditional artist-patron relationship, where creators receive financial support from patrons who believe in their work. Platforms like Patreon and Buy Me a Coffee facilitate patronage for app developers. Here's how to leverage patronage:

1. **Creator Profile**: Create a profile on a patronage platform, showcasing your app development journey, goals, and the value you provide to your supporters.
2. **Tiered Support**: Offer multiple support tiers with varying benefits. Patrons can choose the tier that aligns with their support level and interests.
3. **Exclusive Content**: Provide exclusive content, such as early access to app updates, behind-the-scenes development insights, or special features reserved for patrons.

4. **Community Engagement**: Interact with your patrons through forums, live chats, or Q&A sessions. Building a strong community can encourage ongoing support.
5. **Monthly Support**: Encourage patrons to commit to monthly contributions, providing a stable source of income for your app's development.
6. **Regular Updates**: Keep patrons informed about your progress and how their support contributes to the app's growth.

Choosing the Right Approach

Deciding between crowdfunding and patronage depends on your app's goals and the level of community engagement you desire. Crowdfunding is more suitable for raising a significant amount of initial funds for a specific project, while patronage offers ongoing support and community building.

Both methods require active communication with your supporters. Keep them informed about your app's development, milestones, and how their contributions are making a difference. Building a loyal and engaged community can lead to long-term success and sustainability for your Flutter app.

Section 18.5: Analyzing Revenue and User Engagement

Understanding your app's revenue and user engagement is crucial for making informed decisions about its monetization strategy and future development. In this section, we'll explore how to analyze these key metrics effectively.

Revenue Analysis

Analyzing your app's revenue involves examining the sources of income and how various monetization strategies are performing. Here are some essential steps in revenue analysis:

1. **Revenue Sources**: Identify all revenue sources, including in-app purchases, ads, subscriptions, sponsorships, or any other income streams.
2. **User Segmentation**: Segment your users based on their behavior and spending patterns. This can help tailor your monetization strategies for different user groups.
3. **Conversion Rates**: Analyze conversion rates for different monetization options. For example, determine how many free users upgrade to a premium version or subscribe to your services.
4. **Pricing Optimization**: Evaluate your app's pricing strategy. Consider running A/B tests to find the optimal price point that maximizes revenue without hindering user acquisition.
5. **Ad Performance**: If your app includes advertisements, monitor the performance of ad networks. Measure click-through rates (CTR), fill rates, and revenue per user.
6. **Subscription Metrics**: If you offer subscriptions, track metrics like churn rate, renewal rates, and the lifetime value (LTV) of subscribers.
7. **Payment Methods**: Assess the popularity of different payment methods among your users. Optimize payment processes for convenience and conversion.
8. **Geo-Location Insights**: Understand how revenue varies by geographical location. Adjust pricing or localization to cater to specific markets.
9. **Experimentation**: Continuously experiment with

different revenue models and strategies to find what works best for your app and audience.

User Engagement Analysis

User engagement is a critical metric that directly impacts your app's success. Analyzing user engagement involves assessing how users interact with your app and its content. Here are steps for effective user engagement analysis:

1. **Retention Rates**: Measure user retention rates over time. Identify when and why users stop using your app and take steps to improve retention.
2. **Session Data**: Analyze user sessions, session duration, and the frequency of app use. Determine which features are most engaging and which need improvement.
3. **Feature Usage**: Track which features are popular and which are underutilized. Focus on enhancing and promoting the features that drive engagement.
4. **User Feedback**: Collect user feedback through app reviews, surveys, and support channels. Use this feedback to make informed updates and improvements.
5. **Event Tracking**: Implement event tracking to monitor specific user interactions within your app. This can help you understand user behavior in more detail.
6. **Funnel Analysis**: Create user funnels to analyze the flow of users through key processes or conversion paths in your app. Identify drop-off points and optimize those areas.
7. **Push Notifications**: Evaluate the impact of push notifications on user engagement. Measure open rates and conversion rates for notification campaigns.
8. **User Segmentation**: Segment your user base based on behavior, demographics, or other relevant factors. Tailor

engagement strategies for each segment.

9. **A/B Testing**: Conduct A/B tests to assess the impact of changes on user engagement metrics. This helps you make data-driven decisions.
10. **Benchmarking**: Compare your app's user engagement metrics to industry benchmarks to understand how you stack up against competitors.

Effective revenue and user engagement analysis requires the use of analytics tools and platforms, such as Google Analytics, Firebase Analytics, or third-party solutions tailored for mobile apps. Regularly reviewing and acting upon the insights gained from these analyses will help you refine your app's strategy and ensure its long-term success.

Chapter 19: The Future of Flutter and Dart

Section 19.1: Upcoming Features and Roadmap

Flutter and Dart are continually evolving to meet the ever-changing demands of the mobile development landscape. In this section, we'll delve into the exciting developments and upcoming features in Flutter and Dart, providing you with insights into their future direction.

Flutter's Roadmap

Flutter's development team, led by Google, has a well-defined roadmap that includes several key areas of focus:

1. **Performance Improvements**: Flutter's performance has always been a strong point, but the team is dedicated to making it even better. This includes enhancing the

rendering pipeline, reducing startup times, and optimizing for low-end devices.

2. **Enhanced Developer Tools**: Flutter is known for its rich set of developer tools, including Flutter DevTools. Expect continuous improvements in debugging, profiling, and hot-reloading capabilities.
3. **Platform-Specific Features**: Flutter will continue to bridge the gap between iOS and Android by providing easier access to platform-specific features, such as biometric authentication, augmented reality (AR), and more.
4. **Desktop and Web Support**: Flutter's reach is expanding beyond mobile. Expect improved support for desktop (Windows, macOS, Linux) and web applications, making it a compelling choice for multi-platform development.
5. **Flutter 2.0**: Flutter 2.0 introduced null safety, allowing developers to write safer and more reliable code. Future releases will build upon this foundation to further enhance type safety and code quality.
6. **Internationalization and Accessibility**: Flutter is committed to providing tools and libraries that make it easy to create accessible and internationalized apps. Future updates will focus on improving these aspects.
7. **State Management**: While Flutter offers a range of state management solutions, the community's demand for simpler and more powerful options will lead to the development of new state management libraries and patterns.
8. **Package Ecosystem**: Flutter's package ecosystem is vibrant and growing. The roadmap includes efforts to standardize and improve package quality, ensuring a robust ecosystem for developers.

Dart's Roadmap

Dart, the programming language powering Flutter, has its own roadmap aligned with Flutter's goals:

1. **Sound Null Safety**: Dart's null safety feature, introduced in Dart 2.12, will continue to evolve, ensuring more predictable and safer code.
2. **Dart FFI**: The Foreign Function Interface (FFI) allows Dart code to interoperate with C-based libraries. Expect enhancements and expanded capabilities for Dart FFI.
3. **Dart Web**: Dart is not just for Flutter but also for web development. The roadmap includes improvements in the performance and capabilities of Dart for web applications.
4. **Dart on the Server**: Dart's usage on the server-side for building scalable and efficient backend services is expected to grow. The roadmap will focus on server-side Dart improvements.
5. **Dart's Standard Library**: Dart's standard library will continue to expand with new features and improvements, making it more comprehensive and developer-friendly.
6. **Cross-Platform Compatibility**: Dart aims to be a versatile language that can run efficiently on various platforms. Expect efforts to enhance cross-platform compatibility.
7. **Ecosystem Growth**: Dart's package ecosystem will continue to grow, providing developers with a wealth of libraries and tools to streamline their development workflows.
8. **Language Features**: Dart's language features will evolve based on community feedback and industry trends, ensuring it remains a modern and competitive language.

By staying updated with Flutter and Dart's roadmap and upcoming features, developers can make informed decisions about their technology stack, stay ahead of industry trends, and take full advantage of the capabilities offered by these powerful tools. As the community and ecosystem continue to flourish, exciting opportunities await those who embrace Flutter and Dart for their cross-platform development needs.

Section 19.2: Flutter Beyond Mobile: Expanding Horizons

Flutter's versatility extends beyond mobile app development, opening up new horizons for developers to explore. In this section, we'll discuss how Flutter is being used in various domains, providing examples of its expanding reach.

1. Web Development with Flutter

One of the most significant advancements in Flutter's ecosystem is its capability to create web applications. By compiling Flutter code to JavaScript, developers can build interactive and responsive web apps. Flutter for web benefits from the same rich widget library and hot-reloading features that make Flutter popular for mobile development. Web developers familiar with HTML, CSS, and JavaScript can leverage their skills to create Flutter web applications.

```
import 'package:flutter/material.dart';

void main() {

runApp(MyApp());

}

class MyApp extends StatelessWidget {
```

```
@override
Widget build(BuildContext context) {
return MaterialApp(
home: Scaffold(
appBar: AppBar(
title: Text('Flutter Web Example'),
),
body: Center(
child: Text('Hello, Flutter Web!'),
),
),
);
}
}
```

2. Desktop Applications with Flutter

Flutter is making its mark in desktop application development as well. With Flutter's desktop support, you can create native desktop applications for Windows, macOS, and Linux. This enables developers to maintain a single codebase for both mobile and desktop platforms, reducing development time and effort.

```
import 'package:flutter/material.dart';
import 'package:flutter/widgets.dart';
```

```
void main() {
runApp(MyApp());
}
class MyApp extends StatelessWidget {
@override
Widget build(BuildContext context) {
return MaterialApp(
home: Scaffold(
appBar: AppBar(
title: Text('Flutter Desktop Example'),
),
body: Center(
child: Text('Hello, Flutter Desktop!'),
),
),
);
}
}
```

3. Embedded Systems and IoT

Flutter's lightweight nature and flexibility make it suitable for embedded systems and Internet of Things (IoT) projects. Whether it's building a user interface for a smart appliance or a control panel for a robotics project, Flutter can provide a consistent and visually appealing interface.

```
import 'package:flutter/material.dart';

void main() {

runApp(MyApp());

}

class MyApp extends StatelessWidget {

@override

Widget build(BuildContext context) {

return MaterialApp(

home: Scaffold(

appBar: AppBar(

title: Text('Flutter IoT Example'),

),

body: Center(

child: Text('Hello, Flutter IoT!'),

),

),
```

```
);
}
}
```

4. Embedded Systems and IoT

Flutter's lightweight nature and flexibility make it suitable for embedded systems and Internet of Things (IoT) projects. Whether it's building a user interface for a smart appliance or a control panel for a robotics project, Flutter can provide a consistent and visually appealing interface.

```
import 'package:flutter/material.dart';
void main() {
runApp(MyApp());
}
class MyApp extends StatelessWidget {
@override
Widget build(BuildContext context) {
return MaterialApp(
home: Scaffold(
appBar: AppBar(
title: Text('Flutter IoT Example'),
),
body: Center(
```

```
child: Text('Hello, Flutter IoT!'),
),
),
);
}
}
```

5. Embedded Systems and IoT

Flutter's lightweight nature and flexibility make it suitable for embedded systems and Internet of Things (IoT) projects. Whether it's building a user interface for a smart appliance or a control panel for a robotics project, Flutter can provide a consistent and visually appealing interface.

```
import 'package:flutter/material.dart';
void main() {
runApp(MyApp());
}
class MyApp extends StatelessWidget {
@override
Widget build(BuildContext context) {
return MaterialApp(
home: Scaffold(
appBar: AppBar(
```

```
title: Text('Flutter IoT Example'),
),
body: Center(
child: Text('Hello, Flutter IoT!'),
),
),
);
}
}
```

5. Embedded Systems and IoT

Flutter's lightweight nature and flexibility make it suitable for embedded systems and Internet of Things (IoT) projects. Whether it's building a user interface for a smart appliance or a control panel for a robotics project, Flutter can provide a consistent and visually appealing interface.

```
import 'package:flutter/material.dart';
void main() {
runApp(MyApp());
}
class MyApp extends StatelessWidget {
@override
Widget build(BuildContext context) {
```

```
return MaterialApp(
home: Scaffold(
appBar: AppBar(
title: Text('Flutter IoT Example'),
),
body: Center(
child: Text('Hello, Flutter IoT!'),
),
),
);
}
}
```

6. Game Development

While Flutter is not a dedicated game development framework, its capabilities can be harnessed to create simple games. Developers can use the Flame package, a minimalist game engine for Flutter, to build 2D games. This allows for cross-platform game

Section 19.3: Dart's Evolution and Future Potential

Dart, the programming language behind Flutter, has been evolving steadily since its inception. In this section, we'll explore the evolution of Dart and its future potential, shedding light on how it aligns with the broader tech landscape.

1. The Dart Language Evolution

Dart has seen several updates and releases that have enhanced its features and performance. Some key milestones in Dart's evolution include:

- **Dart 2:** Dart 2 brought significant improvements in terms of language usability, performance, and tooling. The introduction of strong typing with the static keyword and other enhancements made Dart more robust.

- **Null Safety:** Null safety, introduced in Dart 2.12, added a new dimension to Dart's type system. It helps prevent null reference errors, improving code reliability.

- **Sound Null Safety:** Dart's sound null safety is another advancement aimed at making code more predictable and safe. It's a major step forward in ensuring code correctness.

- **Extension Methods:** Dart 2.7 introduced extension methods, allowing developers to add new functionality to existing classes without modifying their source code.

- **Futures and Streams:** Dart's asynchronous programming capabilities, centered around Futures and Streams, continue to be refined and improved for more efficient and expressive code.

2. Dart in the Web Ecosystem

Dart has extended its reach beyond Flutter and is used for web development. Dart for the web leverages technologies like the Dart Dev Compiler (DDC) and can compile to efficient JavaScript code. With its modern features, Dart competes favorably with other web languages.

```
void main() {

print('Hello, Dart for Web!');

}
```

3. Server-Side Dart

Dart can also be used on the server-side. The Dart ecosystem offers frameworks like Aqueduct and Shelf for building web servers and APIs. Server-side Dart is known for its performance and ease of use, making it a viable choice for backend development.

```
import 'dart:io';

void main() {

var server = HttpServer.bind('localhost', 8080);

print('Server started on port 8080');

server.listen((HttpRequest request) {

request.response

..write('Hello from Dart on the server!')

..close();

});
```

```
}
```

4. The Future of Dart

The future of Dart looks promising, with ongoing efforts to improve its ecosystem and align it with industry trends. Some areas of focus include:

- **WebAssembly:** Dart's compatibility with WebAssembly is being explored, which could open up new possibilities for web development.
- **Machine Learning:** Dart is gaining traction in the machine learning community, with libraries like tflite for running TensorFlow Lite models.
- **IoT and Embedded Systems:** Dart's lightweight nature makes it a contender for IoT and embedded systems development.
- **Cross-Platform Compatibility:** Efforts are being made to enhance Dart's compatibility with different platforms and architectures.
- **Community and Adoption:** Dart's success will depend on its adoption and the growth of its community. Collaborative efforts are crucial in shaping Dart's future.

Dart's journey from a language primarily associated with web development to its current role as the driving force behind Flutter demonstrates its adaptability and potential. Developers interested in Dart should keep an eye on its ongoing evolution and the exciting opportunities it offers in the rapidly changing tech landscape.

Section 19.4: Emerging Trends in Cross-Platform Development

As the tech industry continues to evolve, so does the landscape of cross-platform development. In this section, we'll explore some of the emerging trends that are shaping the future of cross-platform development, including how Flutter and Dart are positioned in this changing environment.

1. Convergence of Mobile and Desktop

One of the significant trends in cross-platform development is the convergence of mobile and desktop platforms. Users now expect a seamless experience across various devices, and technologies like Flutter are well-suited to address this demand. Flutter's ability to create apps for mobile, web, and desktop makes it a powerful choice for developers aiming to provide consistent user experiences.

```
import 'package:flutter/material.dart';

void main() {

runApp(MyApp());

}

class MyApp extends StatelessWidget {

@override

Widget build(BuildContext context) {

return MaterialApp(

home: Scaffold(

appBar: AppBar(
```

```
title: Text('Cross-Platform App'),
),
body: Center(
child: Text('Hello, Cross-Platform World!'),
),
),
);
}
}
```

2. Progressive Web Apps (PWAs)

Progressive Web Apps are web applications that offer a native app-like experience on the web. They can be installed on users' devices, work offline, and provide push notifications. Flutter's growing support for web development positions it to be a contender in the PWA space, enabling developers to build PWAs with a single codebase.

3. Augmented Reality (AR) and Virtual Reality (VR)

AR and VR technologies are gaining traction, especially in gaming, education, and training. Flutter's versatility extends to AR and VR development, making it possible to create cross-platform AR and VR applications using libraries like arkit_flutter and google_ar_core.

4. Internet of Things (IoT)

The IoT ecosystem continues to expand, and cross-platform development can play a significant role in building applications that interact with IoT devices. Dart's lightweight nature and potential for running on resource-constrained devices make it a suitable choice for IoT app development.

5. Focus on Performance and Optimization

As cross-platform apps become more prevalent, performance optimization becomes crucial. Flutter's emphasis on performance and the introduction of features like Dart's sound null safety align with the industry's focus on delivering smooth and efficient applications.

6. Collaboration and Open Source

The open-source nature of Flutter and Dart fosters collaboration and innovation. The Flutter community actively contributes to the framework's growth, and this collaborative spirit is a driving force behind its success. Emerging trends often originate from the collective efforts of developers and open-source contributors.

7. App Distribution and Monetization

With cross-platform development gaining ground, considerations around app distribution and monetization are evolving. Developers are exploring new ways to distribute apps, including alternative app stores and progressive web app deployment. Additionally, monetization strategies such as in-app purchases, subscriptions, and advertisements continue to evolve.

8. Ethical and Sustainable Development

In the era of tech ethics and sustainability, cross-platform developers are increasingly mindful of the social and environmental impact of their work. Creating inclusive and accessible apps, reducing energy consumption, and ensuring user privacy are becoming central themes in cross-platform development.

In conclusion, the cross-platform development landscape is evolving rapidly, driven by emerging trends that cater to the changing demands of users and developers. Flutter and Dart are well-positioned to adapt to these trends and continue to play a significant role in shaping the future of cross-platform app development. Developers who stay informed about these trends and incorporate them into their projects will be better equipped to meet the evolving needs of their users and stakeholders.

Section 19.5: Preparing for Future Changes in Technology

As technology continues to advance at an unprecedented pace, it's crucial for developers, especially those in cross-platform development using Flutter and Dart, to prepare for future changes. In this section, we'll discuss strategies and considerations for staying ahead in the ever-evolving tech landscape.

1. Continuous Learning and Skill Development

The most valuable asset for a developer is their skillset. Staying relevant in the field requires continuous learning and skill development. This includes keeping up with the latest updates in Flutter and Dart, exploring new libraries and tools, and adapting to changes in programming paradigms.

```
// Example of continuous learning in Dart

void main() {

print('Never stop learning in Dart!');

}
```

2. Embrace New Technologies

In the tech industry, change is constant. Developers should be open to embracing new technologies that complement their existing skills. For Flutter and Dart developers, this might involve exploring related technologies like Fuchsia, Google's operating system, or diving into emerging fields such as quantum computing.

3. Community Engagement

Active participation in the Flutter and Dart communities is a valuable way to stay informed about upcoming changes and trends. Engaging in forums, attending meetups, and contributing to open-source projects not only keeps you updated but also provides opportunities for networking and collaboration.

4. Experimentation and Prototyping

To adapt to future changes, it's essential to experiment and prototype with new ideas and concepts. Flutter's fast development cycle and hot reload feature make it an excellent platform for rapid prototyping. By experimenting with different approaches, you can discover innovative solutions and stay ahead of the curve.

```
// Example of rapid prototyping in Flutter

void main() {
```

```
runApp(MyApp());
}
class MyApp extends StatelessWidget {
@override
Widget build(BuildContext context) {
return MaterialApp(
home: Scaffold(
appBar: AppBar(
title: Text('Flutter Prototyping'),
),
body: Center(
child: Text('Try, Fail, Learn, Succeed!'),
),
),
);
}
}
```

5. Future-Proofing Code

When writing code, consider future-proofing it by adhering to best practices and design patterns. Writing clean, modular, and well-documented code ensures that your projects remain maintainable and adaptable to future changes or new team members joining the project.

6. Security and Privacy Awareness

As technology evolves, so do security and privacy threats. Developers should stay vigilant and keep their applications secure. Familiarize yourself with best practices for securing user data and be prepared to adapt to new security challenges.

7. Ethical Considerations

In an era of increasing tech ethics awareness, developers must consider the ethical implications of their work. Develop applications that respect user privacy, promote inclusivity, and adhere to ethical guidelines. Consider the potential societal impact of your projects and act responsibly.

8. Environmental Sustainability

Environmental sustainability is gaining importance in tech. Developers should be mindful of the environmental impact of their applications, including energy consumption and resource utilization. Explore ways to optimize your code and make environmentally responsible choices in your projects.

9. Adaptability and Resilience

Lastly, developers must cultivate adaptability and resilience. Technology will continue to evolve, and unexpected challenges may arise. Being adaptable and resilient allows developers to navigate uncertainties and thrive in the face of change.

In conclusion, preparing for future changes in technology is essential for developers working with Flutter and Dart, as well as in the broader tech industry. Continuous learning, embracing new technologies, community engagement, experimentation, future-proofing code, security awareness, ethical considerations, environmental sustainability, and adaptability are all key factors in staying ahead in this dynamic field. By actively addressing these aspects, developers can not only survive but also thrive in the ever-evolving world of technology.

Chapter 20: Final Project: Building a Complete App

Section 20.1: Planning and Designing Your App

Building a complete app is an exciting journey that brings together all the knowledge and skills you've acquired throughout this book. In this final chapter, we'll guide you through the process of planning and designing your app, the first crucial steps in creating a successful project.

1. Define Your App's Purpose and Audience

Before diving into development, it's essential to define your app's purpose and target audience. Ask yourself the following questions:

- What problem does your app solve?
- Who are your potential users?
- What needs or pain points does your app address for them?

Understanding your app's purpose and audience is the foundation upon which you'll build your project.

2. Research and Competitor Analysis

Research is key to a successful app. Study similar apps in the market to identify gaps or areas for improvement. Analyze their features, user experience, and user reviews to gather insights. This information will help you make informed decisions during development.

3. Sketch Your App's User Interface

Start with paper sketches or digital wireframes to outline your app's user interface (UI). Consider the layout, navigation, and placement of elements. This initial sketching phase allows you to visualize the app's structure before diving into code.

4. Create a Feature List

Based on your app's purpose and user needs, create a list of features and functionalities your app will include. Prioritize these features into a minimum viable product (MVP) and additional enhancements.

MVP Features

- User registration and login

- Home screen with essential information

- Basic navigation

- Core functionality

Enhancement Features

- User profiles

- Advanced search

- Social sharing

- In-app purchases

5. Choose the Right Architecture

Selecting the appropriate app architecture is critical. Depending on your project's complexity, consider architectural patterns like MVC,

MVVM, or Clean Architecture. This decision impacts how your code is organized and maintained.

6. Pick Your Development Tools

Choose the development tools and libraries you'll use. In the Flutter ecosystem, this includes state management solutions, navigation packages, and any third-party libraries that align with your project's goals.

7. Set a Realistic Timeline and Milestones

Estimate the time required for each development phase and create a realistic timeline. Break down your project into milestones, allowing you to track progress and make adjustments as needed.

8. Design the User Experience (UX)

Design plays a crucial role in user engagement. Create a visually appealing and intuitive UI that aligns with your app's branding. Consider factors like color schemes, typography, and user interactions.

9. Plan for Testing

Implement a robust testing strategy. This includes unit tests, widget tests, and integration tests to ensure your app functions correctly. Create test cases based on the features you've defined.

10. Prepare for Deployment

Think about how you'll deploy your app. For iOS, you'll need a macOS device for final compilation and submission to the App Store. Android app deployment is more flexible but still requires preparation.

11. Budget and Resources

Consider your budget and available resources. Determine if you'll need additional help, such as designers, QA testers, or backend developers. Allocate resources according to your project's needs.

12. Legal and Compliance

Ensure your app complies with legal requirements, including data privacy regulations and terms of service. Address any copyright or licensing concerns for third-party assets.

13. Backup and Version Control

Implement a version control system (e.g., Git) to track changes and collaborate with team members if applicable. Regularly back up your project to prevent data loss.

14. Project Documentation

Document your project thoroughly. This includes code comments, user guides, and project notes. Documentation helps future developers understand and maintain your app.

15. Seek Feedback

Throughout development, gather feedback from potential users or beta testers. Use their insights to make improvements and refine your app.

16. Stay Agile and Adaptable

Finally, stay agile and adaptable throughout the development process. Be open to changes and adjustments as you gain a better understanding of user needs and market dynamics.

Planning and designing your app are critical steps that lay the foundation for a successful project. Taking the time to define your app's purpose, research competitors, create a feature list, and make informed decisions will set you on the path to building a compelling and valuable application. Once you've completed this planning phase, you'll be ready to move on to implementation and bring your app to life.

Section 20.2: Implementing Core Features and UI

With the planning and design phase completed, it's time to move on to the implementation of your app's core features and user interface (UI). This section will guide you through the process of turning your ideas and sketches into functional code.

1. Set Up Your Development Environment

Ensure you have a well-configured development environment for Flutter. Make sure you have the necessary plugins, extensions, and SDKs installed. You should also set up your version control system to track changes effectively.

2. Create the Project Structure

Organize your project structure according to Flutter's best practices. Typically, this includes folders for assets, lib (source code), test (testing), and any other necessary directories.

```
my_app/
├── assets/
├── lib/
```

```
│ ├── main.dart
│ ├── screens/
│ ├── widgets/
│ └── ...
├── test/
├── pubspec.yaml
└── ...
```

3. Implement Navigation

Start by implementing the app's navigation structure. Define your app's main routes and use Navigator to navigate between screens. You can use packages like fluro or Flutter's built-in routing for this purpose.

4. Build the User Interface

Translate your UI sketches into Flutter widgets. Use a combination of built-in Flutter widgets and custom widgets to create your app's interface. Pay attention to layout, responsiveness, and adherence to your design guidelines.

5. Implement Core Features

Begin implementing the core features of your app. Focus on the MVP features you identified during the planning phase. For example, if your app includes user authentication, set up user registration and login functionality. If it's a productivity app, implement the core task management features.

6. Integrate Backend Services

If your app relies on backend services, integrate them into your project. Use packages like http to make API requests or set up a connection to your server. Ensure proper error handling and data parsing.

7. Manage State Effectively

Choose a state management approach that suits your project. Depending on complexity, you might opt for Provider, Riverpod, Bloc, or another solution. Implement state management to handle app-wide and screen-specific data.

8. Testing and Debugging

Throughout the implementation phase, write unit tests and widget tests to ensure your app behaves as expected. Use Flutter's testing framework to create test cases and detect and fix issues early.

9. Iterate and Refine

As you implement core features and UI elements, continuously test your app on real devices or emulators. Gather feedback from your team, beta testers, or potential users. Be prepared to iterate and refine your app based on this feedback.

10. Performance Optimization

Optimize your app for performance. Profile your app using tools like Flutter DevTools to identify bottlenecks and memory leaks. Implement optimizations to ensure a smooth user experience.

11. Localization and Accessibility

Consider localization if your app targets a global audience. Implement localization and internationalization features to support multiple languages. Ensure your app is accessible to users with disabilities by adhering to accessibility guidelines.

12. Security and Privacy

Pay attention to security and privacy concerns. Protect user data, implement secure authentication, and handle sensitive information carefully. Ensure your app complies with relevant privacy regulations.

13. Documentation

Continuously update your project's documentation. Include code comments, user guides, and API documentation. Well-documented code makes it easier for you and others to understand and maintain the app.

14. Version Control and Collaboration

Keep your codebase in version control to track changes and collaborate effectively. Use branches, pull requests, and code reviews to maintain code quality and consistency.

15. Monitor and Track Errors

Implement error tracking and monitoring tools to identify and resolve issues in your production app. Services like Firebase Crashlytics or Sentry can help you track and fix errors reported by users.

16. Prepare for Testing and Deployment

Before testing on real devices, use emulators and simulators to ensure your app functions on various platforms. Prepare your app for beta testing and deployment on app stores, following their respective guidelines.

17. Finalize MVP and Prepare for Launch

Once you've implemented the MVP features and thoroughly tested your app, finalize your minimum viable product. Address any critical issues and ensure the app meets your quality standards. Prepare for the app's launch by creating marketing materials, app store listings, and promotional strategies.

The implementation phase is where your app starts taking shape. It requires careful attention to detail, constant testing, and a focus on delivering the core functionality defined during the planning phase. As you progress through this phase, you'll inch closer to a fully functional and polished app ready for deployment.

Section 20.3: Integrating Advanced Features

In this section, you'll explore the integration of advanced features into your Flutter app. These features go beyond the basic functionality and can significantly enhance the user experience. While they may not be part of the minimum viable product (MVP), they add value and uniqueness to your application.

1. Push Notifications

Push notifications are a powerful tool to engage users and keep them informed about updates, promotions, or important events related to your app. To implement push notifications in Flutter, you can use packages like Firebase Cloud Messaging (FCM) or OneSignal. Configure your Firebase project, set up the necessary plugins, and handle incoming notifications in your app.

```
// Example of handling incoming notifications with FCM

FirebaseMessaging.onMessage.listen((RemoteMessage message) {

// Handle incoming notification when the app is in the foreground

});

FirebaseMessaging.onMessageOpenedApp.listen((RemoteMessage message) {

// Handle when the user taps the notification and the app is in the background

});
```

2. In-App Purchases

If your app offers premium content, subscriptions, or virtual goods, you can implement in-app purchases. Flutter provides the in_app_purchase package, which allows you to integrate both Android's Play Billing and Apple's StoreKit. Set up product listings, handle purchases, and verify transactions to provide a seamless buying experience.

```
// Example of making an in-app purchase

final ProductDetails product = // Retrieve product details

final PurchaseParam purchaseParam = PurchaseParam(productDetails: product);
```

```
final PurchaseResult purchaseResult = await InAppPurchase.instance.buyNonConsumable(purchaseParam);

if (purchaseResult.status == PurchaseStatus.purchased) {

// Handle successful purchase

}
```

3. Augmented Reality (AR)

AR features can create immersive experiences in your app. With packages like ARKit and ARCore, Flutter allows you to integrate AR into your application. You can build AR-based games, navigation tools, or product visualization features. Be sure to provide clear instructions on how to use AR features to enhance user engagement.

```
// Example of integrating AR with ARCore or ARKit

// ...
```

4. Machine Learning

Machine learning can add intelligent features to your app. Use packages like TensorFlow Lite or ML Kit to implement image recognition, natural language processing, or predictive analytics. You can create apps that classify objects, translate text, or recommend personalized content based on user behavior.

```
// Example of image classification using TensorFlow Lite

// ...
```

5. Biometric Authentication

Enhance security and user convenience by implementing biometric authentication. Flutter provides plugins for fingerprint and face

recognition. Integrate biometric authentication into your login or sensitive transactions to protect user data.

// Example of fingerprint authentication

// ...

6. Augmented Reality (AR)

AR features can create immersive experiences in your app. With packages like ARKit and ARCore, Flutter allows you to integrate AR into your application. You can build AR-based games, navigation tools, or product visualization features. Be sure to provide clear instructions on how to use AR features to enhance user engagement.

// Example of integrating AR with ARCore or ARKit

// ...

7. Machine Learning

Machine learning can add intelligent features to your app. Use packages like TensorFlow Lite or ML Kit to implement image recognition, natural language processing, or predictive analytics. You can create apps that classify objects, translate text, or recommend personalized content based on user behavior.

// Example of image classification using TensorFlow Lite

// ...

8. Biometric Authentication

Enhance security and user convenience by implementing biometric authentication. Flutter provides plugins for fingerprint and face

recognition. Integrate biometric authentication into your login or sensitive transactions to protect user data.

// Example of fingerprint authentication

// ...

9. Augmented Reality (AR)

AR features can create immersive experiences in your app. With packages like ARKit and ARCore, Flutter allows you to integrate AR into your application. You can build AR-based games, navigation tools, or product visualization features. Be sure to provide clear instructions on how to use AR features to enhance user engagement.

// Example of integrating AR with ARCore or ARKit

// ...

10. Machine Learning

Machine learning can add intelligent features to your app. Use packages like TensorFlow Lite or ML Kit to implement image recognition, natural language processing, or predictive analytics. You can create apps that classify objects, translate text, or recommend personalized content based on user behavior.

// Example of image classification using TensorFlow Lite

// ...

11. Biometric Authentication

Enhance security and user convenience by implementing biometric authentication. Flutter provides plugins for fingerprint and face

recognition. Integrate biometric authentication into your login or sensitive transactions to protect user data.

// Example of fingerprint authentication

// ...

12. Augmented Reality (AR)

AR features can create immersive experiences in your app. With packages like ARKit and ARCore, Flutter allows you to integrate AR into your application. You can build AR-based games, navigation tools, or product visualization features. Be sure to provide clear instructions on how to use AR features to enhance user engagement.

// Example of integrating AR with ARCore or ARKit

// ...

13. Machine Learning

Machine learning can add intelligent features to your app. Use packages like TensorFlow Lite or ML Kit to implement image recognition, natural language processing, or predictive analytics. You can create apps that classify objects, translate text, or recommend personalized content based on user behavior.

// Example of image classification using TensorFlow Lite

// ...

14. Biometric Authentication

Enhance security and user convenience by implementing biometric authentication. Flutter provides plugins for fingerprint and face

recognition. Integrate biometric authentication into your login or sensitive transactions to protect user data.

// Example of fingerprint authentication

// ...

15. Augmented Reality (AR)

AR features can create immersive experiences in your app. With packages like ARKit and ARCore, Flutter allows you to integrate AR into your application. You can build AR-based games, navigation tools, or product visualization features. Be sure to provide clear instructions on how to use AR features to enhance user engagement.

// Example of integrating AR with ARCore or ARKit

// ...

16. Machine Learning

Machine learning can add intelligent features to your app. Use packages like TensorFlow Lite or ML Kit to implement image recognition, natural language processing, or predictive analytics. You can create apps that classify objects, translate text, or recommend personalized content based on user behavior.

// Example of image classification using TensorFlow Lite

// ...

17. Biometric Authentication

Enhance security and user convenience by implementing biometric authentication. Flutter provides plugins for fingerprint and face

recognition. Integrate biometric authentication into your login or sensitive transactions to protect user data.

```
// Example of fingerprint authentication

// ...
```

18. Augmented Reality (AR)

AR features can create immersive experiences in your app. With packages like ARKit and ARCore, Flutter allows you to integrate AR into your application. You can build AR-based games, navigation tools, or product visualization features. Be sure

---

Section 20.4: Testing and Refining Your App

Testing and refining your Flutter app is a crucial step before its launch. This phase ensures that your application is robust, user-friendly, and free of critical bugs. In this section, we'll discuss the essential aspects of testing and refining your app.

1. Unit Testing

Unit tests are vital for verifying that individual functions, classes, or methods in your app work correctly. Flutter provides the test package for writing unit tests. You can create tests that cover various scenarios and use cases to validate the behavior of your code.

```
// Example of a unit test in Flutter

test('Addition function should return the correct result', () {

expect(add(2, 3), 5);

});
```

2. Widget Testing

Widget tests focus on the user interface (UI) components of your app. With Flutter's flutter_test package, you can write widget tests to ensure that your widgets render correctly and respond to user interactions as expected. Widget tests simulate user interactions and validate the widget tree.

```
// Example of a widget test in Flutter

testWidgets('Counter increments smoke test', (WidgetTester tester) async {

// Build our app and trigger a frame.

await tester.pumpWidget(MyApp());

// Verify that our counter starts at 0.

expect(find.text('0'), findsOneWidget);

expect(find.text('1'), findsNothing);

// Tap the '+' icon and trigger a frame.

await tester.tap(find.byIcon(Icons.add));

await tester.pump();

// Verify that our counter has incremented.

expect(find.text('0'), findsNothing);

expect(find.text('1'), findsOneWidget);

});
```

3. Integration Testing

Integration tests evaluate how different parts of your app work together. They ensure that various widgets, screens, or components collaborate correctly. Flutter provides the integration_test package for writing integration tests. These tests can help identify issues that may arise from the interaction between different parts of your app.

```
// Example of an integration test in Flutter

void main() {

testWidgets('Counter increments when the floating action button is pressed',

(WidgetTester tester) async {

await tester.pumpWidget(MyApp());

expect(find.text('0'), findsOneWidget);

expect(find.text('1'), findsNothing);

await tester.tap(find.byIcon(Icons.add));

await tester.pump();

expect(find.text('0'), findsNothing);

expect(find.text('1'), findsOneWidget);

});

}
```

4. User Acceptance Testing (UAT)

User acceptance testing involves real users who explore your app and provide feedback. It's an essential step to ensure that your app meets the needs and expectations of your target audience. Gather feedback, address usability issues, and make necessary improvements based on user input.

5. Performance Testing

Performance testing evaluates your app's speed, responsiveness, and resource consumption. Use profiling tools like the Flutter DevTools to identify performance bottlenecks, memory leaks, or slow rendering. Optimize your app to provide a smooth and lag-free user experience.

6. Usability Testing

Usability testing assesses how intuitive and user-friendly your app is. Invite users to perform specific tasks within your app while observing their interactions. Identify areas where users struggle or encounter confusion and make design and usability improvements accordingly.

7. Accessibility Testing

Ensure that your app is accessible to users with disabilities. Use accessibility tools and perform tests to verify that your app's UI elements, navigation, and content are accessible through screen readers and other assistive technologies. Address accessibility issues to make your app more inclusive.

8. Beta Testing

Before the official release, conduct beta testing with a select group of users. Distribute a beta version of your app and collect feedback on real-world usage. Beta testing helps identify last-minute issues, compatibility problems, and user feedback that can shape your final release.

9. Continuous Refinement

Iterate on your app based on the feedback received during testing phases. Continuously refine and enhance your app's features, performance, and user experience. Regularly update your app to address bugs, security vulnerabilities, and evolving user expectations.

10. Documentation and User Support

Provide comprehensive documentation and user support resources. Include user guides, FAQs, and contact information for user assistance. A well-documented app and responsive support can improve user satisfaction and reduce support requests.

By thoroughly testing and refining your Flutter app, you increase its chances of success in the competitive app market. A robust, user-friendly, and bug-free application is more likely to attract and retain users, ultimately contributing to its long-term success.

Section 20.5: Launching and Marketing Your App

Launching and marketing your Flutter app is a critical phase that determines its success and reach in the market. After putting in extensive effort in development and testing, it's time to introduce your app to the world. This section discusses strategies and steps to effectively launch and market your app.

1. App Store Submission

One of the primary steps in launching your app is submitting it to the respective app stores, such as the Apple App Store for iOS and Google Play for Android. Follow the guidelines and requirements of each platform carefully to ensure a smooth submission process. Prepare all necessary assets, including app icons, screenshots, and descriptions.

// Example: Preparing assets for app store submission

flutter build ios—release

flutter build apk—release

2. App Store Optimization (ASO)

Optimize your app's listing on app stores to improve its visibility and discoverability. This includes using relevant keywords, writing compelling descriptions, and creating eye-catching app icons and screenshots. ASO helps increase your app's chances of appearing in search results and getting downloaded.

// Example: Optimizing app store listing

- Choose relevant keywords for your app's description.

- Highlight unique features and benefits.

- Create visually appealing screenshots and icons.

3. Social Media Presence

Leverage social media platforms to create a buzz around your app. Share updates, teasers, and behind-the-scenes content to engage with your audience. Create official social media profiles for your app and use targeted advertising to reach potential users.

// Example: Sharing app updates on social media

- Regularly post about your app's development progress.

- Use social media advertising to reach a broader audience.

- Engage with users through comments and messages.

4. App Website and Landing Page

Build a website or landing page dedicated to your app. Include information about its features, benefits, and a download link. A well-designed website can serve as a central hub for potential users to learn more about your app.

// Example: Creating a website for your app

- Register a domain name related to your app's name.

- Use website builders or templates for easy development.

- Include download links for different app stores.

5. Email Marketing

Collect email addresses from interested users and create an email marketing campaign. Send out newsletters, updates, and exclusive offers to build and maintain a user base. Email marketing can be a powerful tool for user retention and re-engagement.

// Example: Setting up an email marketing campaign

- Use email capture forms on your website and app.

- Send personalized emails based on user interactions.

- Provide value through informative content and promotions.

6. Influencer Collaborations

Partner with influencers or bloggers who have a relevant audience. They can provide authentic reviews and endorsements, reaching a wider user base. Choose influencers whose audience aligns with your app's target demographic.

// Example: Collaborating with influencers

- Identify influencers in your app's niche.

- Reach out for collaborations or sponsored posts.

- Provide them with early access to your app for reviews.

7. App Launch Event

Organize a launch event or webinar to introduce your app to the public. A launch event can generate excitement and interest in your app. Consider offering limited-time promotions or discounts during the launch period to encourage downloads.

// Example: Hosting an app launch event

- Schedule a live stream or webinar to showcase your app.

- Invite industry experts or guest speakers for insights.

- Offer exclusive app access or rewards to attendees.

8. User Feedback and Iteration

After the initial launch, pay close attention to user feedback and reviews. Continuously iterate on your app based on user suggestions and bug reports. A responsive development approach can lead to higher user satisfaction and app ratings.

// Example: Listening to user feedback

- Monitor app store reviews and respond to user comments.

- Collect feedback through in-app surveys or contact forms.

- Prioritize and implement user-requested features.

9. Analytics and Metrics

Use analytics tools to track user behavior, app performance, and marketing effectiveness. Understand user engagement, retention, and conversion rates. Data-driven insights can help you refine your marketing strategy and improve your app.

// Example: Using analytics tools

- Implement analytics SDKs like Firebase Analytics.

- Monitor user acquisition sources and conversion funnels.

- Adjust marketing efforts based on performance data.

10. Continuous Marketing Efforts

App marketing is an ongoing process. Keep marketing your app through various channels, including social media, content creation, and advertising. Stay updated with industry trends and user preferences to adapt your marketing strategies.

// Example: Sustaining marketing efforts

- Create regular content, such as blog posts or videos.

- Explore new advertising platforms and opportunities.

- Stay engaged with your app's user community.

Launching and marketing your Flutter app requires a strategic approach and continuous effort. By following these steps and adapting your strategies based on real-world feedback and data, you can increase your app's visibility, user base, and overall success in the competitive app market.

www.ingramcontent.com/pod-product-compliance
Lightning Source LLC
LaVergne TN
LVHW090257210926
848480LV00001B/56
* 9 7 9 8 2 2 4 1 5 4 1 0 4 *